Orchids

Orchids

WILMA AND BRIAN RITTERSHAUSEN

EDITED BY CAROLE MCGLYNN

Photographs by Linda Burgess

Quadrille

First published in 2005 by
Quadrille Publishing Limited
Alhambra House,
27-31 Charing Cross Road,
London WC2H 0LS

Creative Director: Helen Lewis
Editorial Director: Jane O' Shea
Art Editor: Chalkley Calderwood Pratt
Editor: Carole McGlynn
Production: Rebecca Short

Based on material originally published in *Orchids*, A
practical guide to the world's most fascinating plants

British Library Cataloguing-in-Publication Data
A catalogue record for this book is available
from the British Library.

ISBN 1-84400-198-9

Printed in China

Contents

Introduction

Orchids are the largest and most diverse flowering plant family on earth, found in conditions varying from deserts to tropical rainforests. Once the preserve of intrepid plant hunters, today's mass production worldwide has made these fascinating plants available to everyone. All the orchids shown in this book are readily found and easy to care for in the home, where their exquisite blooms will give years of pleasure in return for a minimum of attention.

What makes orchids special?

Most tropical orchids are epiphytic in the wild – that is, they grow on the trunks and branches of trees. They are not parasitic but have adopted trees as their home to be closer to light and fresh air. They absorb moisture from the air through aerial roots, without harming the tree. They are more diverse than terrestrial orchids – which grow in the ground – especially in their flowers, the most colourful, flamboyant blooms being found in equatorial forests.

Epiphytic orchids make one of two types of growth. Some have pseudobulbs, which vary in shape and size, while others have thick, succulent foliage. Pseudobulbs are swollen stems used for water storage. They may be round, conical or elongated into long stems or 'canes', depending on the genus. They are joined together by a hard, woody rhizome. New pseudobulbs are added each growing season, increasing the plant's size. Each psuedobulb, supported by an extensive root system, can have one or many leaves, which may be long and narrow or short and thickened. Blooms are produced annually on flower spikes which grow from either the base or the top of the pseudobulb.

Those orchids with thick, succulent foliage, including *Phalaenopsis*, have a single upward-growing rhizome. New leaves are produced from the centre until a fan of foliage is built up. The substantial leaves retain moisture as the pseudobulbs do.

The flowers

Orchid flowers are produced on flower spikes which may arise from the base of the plant or the tip of the pseudobulb. The flower spikes carry from one to several dozen flowers, ranging extensively in size, shape, colouring and texture. But they all conform to a basic pattern which defines the plant as an orchid. Each flower has an outer whorl, consisting of three sepals, and an inner whorl, made up of two lateral petals with a third in between, modified to form the lip. Most orchids are pollinated by insects and the lip's role is to signal to a passing pollinator. It also serves as a landing platform for visiting insects, attracted by its vividly coloured markings. Cross-pollination between species has led to some natural hybrids in the wild but,

more significantly, has been exploited by breeders over two centuries to produce today's ever-increasing number of man-made orchid hybrids.

Growing in the home

The key to growing orchids at home is to provide conditions close to those of their original habitat. They divide into three groups according to temperature needs.

Cool-growing orchids, living at high altitudes in the wild, include *Cymbidium, Odontoglossum, Coelogyne, Encyclia* and some dendrobiums. All grow well indoors provided they are not exposed to extremes of temperature such as a hot conservatory or a room left unheated in winter. Choose a well-lit part of a living room which is not directly in the sun; it should be warm by day and cool at night.

Intermediate orchids include the fabulous tropical cattleyas, the warmer-growing slipper orchids and *Miltoniopsis*. Grow cattleyas in a warm room in good light, with background heat overnight in winter. Slipper orchids and *Miltoniopsis* need a slightly shadier position.

Warm-growing orchids, including moth orchids (*Phalaenopsis*) originating from the forested tropics of the Philippines, need a warm but shady position where they can be kept moist. They also need warm temperatures at night but should not be placed too close to a heat source, such as a radiator.

Cymbi

diums

Cymbidiums are leafy evergreen plants that stand over 90cm (3ft) in bloom. The waxy flowers last up to ten weeks, brightening the dull winter months. Growing cymbidiums is not hard, provided they are given a position of light shade in summer and full light in winter, watering less in winter. Once the flower spikes become visible, in early summer, tie them to a thin cane; after flowering, cut them off 2.5cm (1in) from the base. Artificial heating is needed in winter to maintain a healthy temperature no lower than 10°C (50°F) at night, and rising by at least 3-4°C (10°F) in the day.

Cymbidium **Mini Sarah 'Sunburst'**

With a pretty yellow-spotted lip, this is
one of a range of compact orchids
produced to give a shorter plant with small
flowers, for indoor use. Several flower
spikes can be produced in a season, not
all opening at once, giving an extended
season of bloom. Flowering can carry on
well into spring, during which time the
plant needs regular watering and feeding
to maintain the extra effort required.
Repot as soon as possible after flowering.

FLOWER 9cm (3½in) wide
FLOWER SPIKE 60cm (24in) long
PLANT SIZE 75cm (30in) high
POT SIZE 20cm (8in)
TEMPERATURE Cool

Cymbidium **Bruttera**

This attractive compact hybrid is among the first to bloom after the summer growing season. Free-flowering through autumn, it carries a refreshing fragrance to complement its clear colouring: a medium-sized plant can have up to 6 flower spikes. To ensure a good crop of flowers, place outdoors in summer to produce harder growth. Bring it back indoors into a light position once you see the spikes, resembling fat pencils, at the base of the plant.

FLOWER
5cm (2in) wide

FLOWER SPIKE
90cm (36in) long

PLANT SIZE
75cm (30in) high

POT SIZE
15cm (6in)

TEMPERATURE
Cool

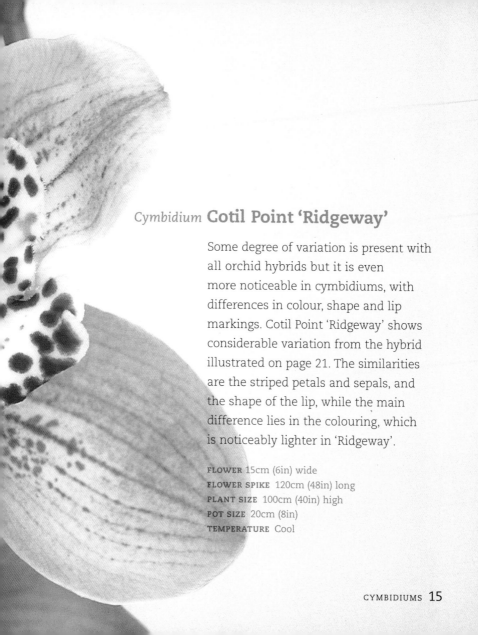

Cymbidium **Cotil Point 'Ridgeway'**

Some degree of variation is present with all orchid hybrids but it is even more noticeable in cymbidiums, with differences in colour, shape and lip markings. Cotil Point 'Ridgeway' shows considerable variation from the hybrid illustrated on page 21. The similarities are the striped petals and sepals, and the shape of the lip, while the main difference lies in the colouring, which is noticeably lighter in 'Ridgeway'.

FLOWER 15cm (6in) wide
FLOWER SPIKE 120cm (48in) long
PLANT SIZE 100cm (40in) high
POT SIZE 20cm (8in)
TEMPERATURE Cool

Cymbidium **Maureen Grapes 'Marilyn'**

This fresh, spring green orchid has retained all the hues from the original species, *Cymbidium ensiflorum*. The sweet fragrance has continued through this special breeding line, developed in New Zealand to fill a gap in the cymbidium flowering season. The dense red peppering on the lip is also indicative of the species. 'Marilyn' is sequential flowering, with spikes developing at different stages to give a succession of blooms over a long period (see also photograph on page 5).

FLOWER
5cm (2in) wide

FLOWER SPIKE
90cm (36in) long

PLANT SIZE
75cm (30in) high

POT SIZE
15cm (6in)

TEMPERATURE
Cool

Cymbidium **Bethlehem**

This white, midwinter-flowering Californian-bred hybrid has the slightest blush of pink touching the sepals, while the petals carry a light adornment, highlighted in greater detail on the prettily marked lip. To ensure the plant blooms well the following year, place out of doors for the summer months to produce a strong growth which will ripen well before producing its flower spikes.

FLOWER
12cm (5in) wide

FLOWER SPIKE
120cm (48in) long

PLANT SIZE
100cm (40in) high

POT SIZE
20cm (8in)

TEMPERATURE
Cool

Cymbidium **Cotil Point**

Cotil Point is an eye-catching hybrid, bred in Jersey in the late 1990s, one of the latest in a long line of superb red-flowered hybrids giving a wonderful depth of colour with striping on the petals and sepals. It is winning awards on both sides of the Atlantic and has already gained three awards of merit from the Royal Horticultural Society. The large flowers open during winter and can be left on the plant, or cut singly.

FLOWER
15cm (6in) wide

FLOWER SPIKE
120cm (48in) long

PLANT SIZE
100cm (40in) high

POT SIZE
20cm (8in)

TEMPERATURE
Cool

Cymbidium **Glowing Valley 'Sunrise'**

This lovely hybrid was raised in 1985 from the finest Australian stock. The perfectly shaped flower has a hint of shell pink with a delicately spotted lip, creating a subtle counterpoint to the bolder colourings found among cymbidiums. The very pale coloured flowers can be spoilt by too much bright light and, while they are in bloom, they should be kept away from direct sunlight, when they will last in perfection for up to ten weeks.

FLOWER 9cm (3½in) wide
FLOWER SPIKE 120cm (48in) long
PLANT SIZE 100cm (40in) high
POT SIZE 20cm (8in)
TEMPERATURE Cool

Cymbidium **Tangerine Mary**

Raised in New Zealand, this winter-flowering cymbidium is a breakthrough into the vibrant colours once seen only in the later, mid-season hybrids. The plant is compact, with its leaves held upright, and demands less space than most cymbidiums. The flower spikes carry numerous flowers, held naturally upright and reaching no taller than the foliage. A mature plant blooms freely all winter, producing a succession of flower spikes.

FLOWER
5cm (2in) wide

FLOWER SPIKE
90cm (36in) long

PLANT SIZE
60cm (24in) high

POT SIZE
15cm (6in) high

TEMPERATURE
Cool

Cymbidium **Valley Splash 'Awesome'**

Australia has become the breeding centre of the world for many of the best *Cymbidium* hybrids. All those with 'Valley' in their name are from Valley Orchids in South Australia; Valley Splash appeared in 1991. The brushed petals and sepals on this lovely hybrid give an unusual large, bi-coloured, slightly cupped flower reminiscent of a watercolour in its delicacy. Up to 12 waxy blooms are produced on an upright flower spike taller than the foliage; they last 8-10 weeks in winter.

FLOWER
10cm (4in) wide

FLOWER SPIKE
120cm (48in) long

PLANT SIZE
100cm (40in) high

POT SIZE
20cm (8in)

TEMPERATURE
Cool

Cymbidium **Nevada**

Cymbidiums such as this superb yellow hybrid have been cultivated and hybridized for over 100 years. This modern hybrid produces long, upright flower spikes in spring, each with a dozen or more blooms lasting for weeks. As the stems lengthen, they need support to prevent them snapping under their own weight. They require plenty of headroom but can spend the summer outside to benefit from extra light to encourage the flowers.

FLOWER
10cm (4in) wide

FLOWER SPIKE
120cm (48in) long

PLANT SIZE
90cm (36in) high

POT SIZE
30cm (12in)

TEMPERATURE
Cool

Cymbidium **Summer Pearl 'Sonya'**

'Sonya' is an attractive, miniature, white form of the popular fragrant hybrid, Summer Pearl. This hybrid comes in a range of colours and extends flowering into the summer months. 'Sonya' is very often slightly fragrant; this is most noticeable on a warm, sunny morning.

FLOWER 8cm (3in) wide
FLOWER SPIKE 90cm (36in) long
PLANT SIZE 60cm (24in) high
POT SIZE 20cm (8in)
TEMPERATURE Cool

Cymbidium **Valley Blush 'Magnificent'**

This cymbidium is easily able to produce up to a dozen large, dramatic flowers per spike, each with clear, spring-green colouring and a delicately spotted lip. Several spikes appear on a large plant. The green-flowered hybrids require good light to initiate the flower spikes in late summer but, once the buds begin to show, they should be given more shade. Once in bloom, keep the plant in shade to prolong flowering and maintain colour.

FLOWER
10cm (4in) wide

FLOWER SPIKE
120cm (48in) long

PLANT SIZE
100cm (40in) high

POT SIZE
20cm (8in)

TEMPERATURE
Cool

Odontog
alliance

Odontoglossums and the numerous natural and specially bred genera related to them are decorative and easy to grow. These evergreen plants produce green pseudobulbs and two pairs of flexible leaves, while the flower spikes may carry 5-100 dainty, long-lasting blooms at almost any time of year. There is a broad colour range and a multitude of patterns. These orchids enjoy a shady position and should be watered all year round. They can be grown on the cooler side, at a minimum temperature of 10°C (50°F) and a general maximum of 24°C (75°F).

lossum

Odontoglossum **Geyser Gold**

Raised in New Zealand in 1989, this yellow hybrid inherits its distinctive light colouring from its species grandparent, *Lemboglossum (Odontoglossum) bictoniense* var. *alba*. The pale yellow base is heavily overlaid with deeper yellow blotching, producing a ripple effect of light and dark. The individual blooms are less rounded than many modern hybrids, giving a well-defined outline and crisp edges. Up to 12 flowers are carried on a long spike, mostly in autumn. This smaller plant is easy to grow and flower.

FLOWER
5cm (2in) wide

FLOWER SPIKE
50cm (20in) long

PLANT SIZE
30cm (12in) high

POT SIZE
10cm (4in)

TEMPERATURE
Cool

Odontioda **Marie Noel 'Bourgogyne'**

The most highly patterned orchids of all are found among the *Odontoglossum* hybrids. *Oda.* Marie Noel has won many awards for outstanding quality and 'Bourgogyne' is one of the finest forms, with its distinctive leopard spotting on the flowers. The parent species come from the Andean mountains of South America where they grow on trees at high altitudes, enjoying cool nights and mountain breezes. The well-rounded blooms, with sepals and petals of equal size, have a neat lip.

FLOWER
6cm (2½in) wide

FLOWER SPIKE
30cm (12in) long

PLANT SIZE
30cm (12in) high

POT SIZE
10cm (4in)

TEMPERATURE
Cool

Odontonia **Boussole 'Blanche'**

Here is a French-bred intergeneric hybrid of exceptional quality, a result of crossing *Miltoniopsis* with *Odontoglossum*. The star-shaped flowers with pointed petals can be traced back to the species *O. crispum*, which produced all modern white hybrids. The flared lip and slight pink tinge on the inside of the flower come from its pink-flowered parent, *Miltonia vexillaria*; the coloration is deeper on the outside.

FLOWER
8cm (3in) wide

FLOWER SPIKE
30cm (12in) long

PLANT SIZE
30cm (12in) high

POT SIZE
10cm (4in)

TEMPERATURE
Cool

Odontocidium **Hansueli Isler**

The brilliant patterning and colourful arrangement of red-brown overlaid on a yellow base even shines through the buds of this delightful, German-bred hybrid. Several modern hybrids are named to honour members of the Swiss Isler family of commercial growers. This plant, with its ornate lip, is very free-flowering; it produces sturdy, upright spikes with 6-10 blooms per stem. These are long-lasting but need to be kept out of direct sun or excessive heat while in bloom.

FLOWER
6cm (2½in) wide

FLOWER SPIKE
50cm (20in) long

PLANT SIZE
30cm (12in) high

POT SIZE
10cm (4in)

TEMPERATURE
Cool

Oncidium **Star Wars**

Oncidiums are typically, but not always, yellow flowered. This is a delightful example of a modern hybrid bred from Brazilian species. Most oncidiums exhibit a large, flared lip, as seen here, dwarfing the lesser, lightly barred sepals and petals. Many blooms appear on side branches to the main flower spike.

FLOWER
5cm (2in) wide

FLOWER SPIKE
60cm (24in) long

PLANT SIZE
40cm (16in) high

POT SIZE
15cm (6in)

TEMPERATURE
Cool

Oncidium **Sharry Baby 'Sweet Fragrance'**

Yellow is the predominant colour among oncidiums, but by no means all are yellow. This lovely Hawaiian-bred hybrid has flowers which show deep red colouring, accompanied by a strong chocolate fragrance. The pretty, well-defined lip has a pinched middle and flared base found in *Oncidium ornithorhynchum* (see page 52). The numerous flowers are produced on side branches on the spike, which can be trained upright or allowed to arch naturally.

FLOWER
2cm (1in) wide

FLOWER SPIKE
60cm (24in) long

PLANT SIZE
25cm (10in) high

POT SIZE
15cm (6in)

TEMPERATURE
Cool

Oncidium flexuosum

This Brazilian species was introduced in 1821. Its narrow petals and sepals, lightly barred with brown, are insignificant compared to the exaggerated deep yellow lip. Given the fanciful name of 'dancing ladies', the lips resemble swirling skirts as the orchids dance in a gentle wind. The small flowers appear in autumn at the end of a long spike, on branches which create a shower effect. The pseudobulbs, produced at intervals, have a length of rhizome in between, so it is best grown on a piece of cork bark, or in a 12cm (5in) pot up a mossy pole.

FLOWER
2cm (1in) wide

FLOWER SPIKE
60cm (24in) long

PLANT SIZE
50cm (20in) high

POT SIZE
12cm (5in)

TEMPERATURE
Cool

Oncidium ornithorhynchum

This pretty species from Mexico and Guatemala, first described in 1815, is still widely grown today. The name derives from the Greek, meaning 'beak of a bird' – a reference to the replica of a tiny dove's head at the bloom's centre. Its strongly fragrant, rosy pink flowers are numerous on the compact flowering spikes; the individual blooms are beautifully formed. The flowers appear in autumn, after which the plant has a brief rest. Keep out of direct sun.

FLOWER
2cm (1in) wide

FLOWER SPIKE
20cm (8in) long

PLANT SIZE
20cm (8in) high

POT SIZE
10cm (4in)

TEMPERATURE
Cool

Odontobrassia **Aztec**

This new hybrid is one of the novelty crosses within the highly variable *Odontoglossum* group. As yet unnamed, it carries the parents' names for identification; *Brassia* Stardust is a long-petalled, green-flowered spider orchid. Though it needs light shade in summer, this charming cross will tolerate a slightly higher maximum temperature of 30°C (85°F). These hybrids usually have a rest period in winter, when they can be kept on the dry side in full light until new growth is seen.

FLOWER 5cm (2in) wide
FLOWER SPIKE 45cm (18in) long
PLANT SIZE 30cm (12in) high
POT SIZE 12cm (5in)
TEMPERATURE Cool

Sanderara **Rippon Tor 'Burnham'**

This hybrid between three genera is produced by crossing *Odontoglossum*, *Brassia* and *Cochlioda*; it is named after the founder of a famous nursery – Sander & Sons of St Albans, England. The first *Sanderara* was registered in 1937. The flowers are produced on a tall, arching stem with up to 12 large blooms. The ivory-white base is overlaid with splashes of red and pink, intensified at the centre of the cream-yellow lip. The plant is tall, robust and it blooms mostly during spring.

FLOWER
8cm (3in) wide

FLOWER SPIKE
50cm (20in) long

PLANT SIZE
25cm (10in) high

POT SIZE
15cm (6in)

TEMPERATURE
Cool

Burrageara **Stefan Isler**

Four popular genera have combined to produce this richly coloured hybrid, an eye-catching creation of reds and light reds. *Miltonia* influenced the dramatic lip, while *Cochlioda* gives the flower its colouring. The flower size has been slightly reduced by *Oncidium* and the whole plant is quite compact. The blooms, with vivid sepals and petals, have a contrasting fiddle-shaped orange lip. Carried on side branches to the main stem, they last weeks and can be produced at any time of year.

FLOWER
6cm (2½in) wide

FLOWER SPIKE
60cm (24in) long

PLANT SIZE
23cm (9in) high

POT SIZE
15cm (6in)

TEMPERATURE
Cool

Aspasia lunata

This is a small, lesser-known species in the *Odontoglossum* alliance, more closely related to *Brassia*, grown for its attractive blooms. It produces small, lengthened pseudobulbs with a pair of narrow leaves and quickly establishes itself as a specimen if left undivided for a few years. It may be grown in a pot or a hanging basket. The early summer flowers are carried on shortened spikes, with a single star-shaped bloom; the petals and sepals are narrow and the lip is flared.

FLOWER
5cm (2in) wide

PLANT SIZE
15cm (6in) high

POT SIZE
12cm (5in)

TEMPERATURE
Cool

Vuylstekeara **Cambria 'Plush'**

This is probably the most popular orchid
in the *Odontoglossum* alliance, due to its
large, strikingly beautiful, flamboyant
flowers, its willingness to bloom and its
ease of growing. *Vuyl.* Cambria first
appeared in 1931; its popularity spread
worldwide and today it is found in every
country where orchids are cultivated. It
will bloom twice a year, often producing
two spikes from one pseudobulb, with
up to 12 long-lasting blooms on each.
Do not allow the pseudobulbs to shrivel.

FLOWER
8cm (3in) wide

FLOWER SPIKE
50cm (20in) long

PLANT SIZE
30cm (12in) high

POT SIZE
10cm (4in)

TEMPERATURE
Cool

Vuylstekeara **Cambria 'Yellow'**

Here is the yellow variety of *Vuyl.* Cambria 'Plush' (page 65). During the mass cloning process, tissue-coloured variants were accidentally produced. One of these, 'Yellow', appeared a few years ago in Holland and has since gone on to reproduce true to its colour; this freak occurrence has made the plant very popular. In all other respects Cambria 'Yellow' is identical to Cambria 'Plush'.

FLOWER
8cm (3in) wide

FLOWER SPIKE
50cm (20in) long

PLANT SIZE
30cm (12in) high

POT SIZE
10cm (4in)

TEMPERATURE
Cool

Wilsonara **Widecombe Fair**

FLOWER
5cm (2in) wide

FLOWER SPIKE
90cm (36in) long

PLANT SIZE
23cm (9in) high

POT SIZE
15cm (6in)

TEMPERATURE
Cool

This captivating hybrid is the result of using different species within the *Odontoglossum* alliance to give a smaller, more open style of flower. While the plant is typical of odontoglossums, the flower spike is taller, carrying numerous flowers on side branches. The summer-flowering spikes take months to develop their blooms and need supporting from a young age. This vigorous hybrid will grow just as well in a warmer environment of 13°C (55°F) minimum, if daytime temperatures are kept below 24°C (75°F).

Wilsonara **Uruapan 'Tyron'**

Wilsonara is the result of crossing three natural genera, *Cochlioda, Oncidium* and *Odontoglossum*. The cross is named after Gurney Wilson, an eminent orchidist and writer of the early 20th century. Very few new wilsonaras were raised after 1916 until the introduction of *Oncidium tigrinum* revitalized the genus, creating wonderfully rich combinations as seen in this beautiful symmetrical flower. A strong, robust grower, it produces tall flower spikes with up to 12 blooms per stem. Its flowering season varies throughout the year.

FLOWER
9cm (3½in) wide

FLOWER SPIKE
50cm (20in) long

PLANT SIZE
25cm (10in) high

POT SIZE
15cm (6in)

TEMPERATURE
Cool

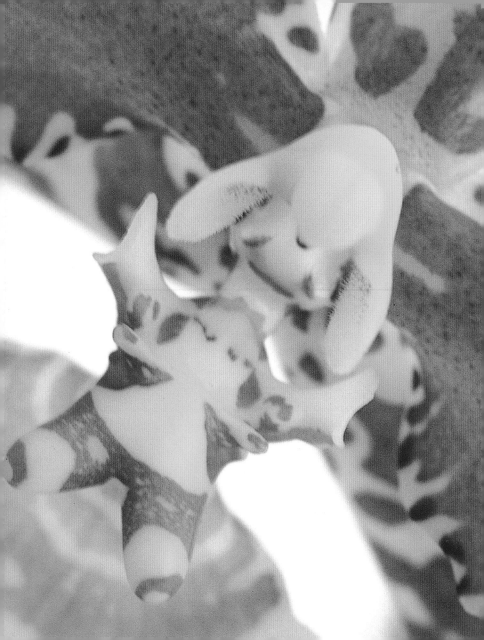

Rossioglossum grande

This Guatemalan species is known as the clown orchid, referring to the life-like shape at the centre of the flower. This part of the central lip formation guides the insect to the pollen, hidden behind the anther at the end of the column, here resembling a clown's oversized head. The plant is related to *Odontoglossum*, although the huge, glossy chestnut and yellow flower is unique in the orchid family. The blooms are produced, several on an arching spike, during the autumn, and they last up to 3 weeks.

FLOWER
12cm (5in) wide

FLOWER SPIKE
30cm (12in) long

PLANT SIZE
30cm (12in) high

POT SIZE
15cm (6in)

TEMPERATURE
Cool

Milton

iopsis

The beautiful pansy orchids have huge, flat blooms with a radiant 'mask' decoration on the lip and a honey fragrance. Very free-flowering, they peak in early summer and autumn. They enjoy a shady area indoors, given some humidity from a tray of wet pebbles, and should be kept evenly moist at the roots all year, with light feeding in summer. The soft leaves are easily  marked, so do not spray the plants overhead. Though cool-growing, they are happy in slightly warmer conditions, with a minimum of 12°C (54°F) and a maximum of 25° (77°F).

Miltoniopsis **St Helier 'Plum'**

'Plum' is one of the colourful Jersey-bred *Miltoniopsis* St Helier line, whose bold, decorative designs include a butterfly-shaped mask at the centre of the flower. This illustrates the variation that can occur with the same hybrid but different individual clones (see also 'Pink Delight', page 92). Raised in 1989, this is one of the best miltoniopsis, with the exquisite patterning at the centre of its flower.

FLOWER
10cm (4in) wide

FLOWER SPIKE
23cm (9in) long

PLANT SIZE
30cm (12in) high

POT SIZE
12cm (5in)

TEMPERATURE
Cool

Miltoniopsis **Cindy Kane x Beethoven**

The patterning on this highly individual flower has become subtle on the petals, with striking veining on the sepals.

The lip carries the lovely 'waterfall' design which can be traced back through many generations to the species *M. phalaenopsis*. This patterning is much sought after and not always obtainable in such a defined manner. Expect to pay more for hybrids with this decoration, which is seen mainly in the pink and red varieties.

FLOWER
10cm (4in) wide

FLOWER SPIKE
23cm (9in) long

PLANT SIZE
30cm (12in) high

POT SIZE
12cm (5in) high

TEMPERATURE
Cool

Miltoniopsis **Eureka**

This lovely, clear yellow *Miltoniopsis* is an outstanding hybrid with soft, buttery tones. Of American origin; it was raised in 1980, one of the latest in a successful line producing the elusive yellow colouring. With twice-yearly blooms from a modest-sized plant, it is an ideal first orchid, offering good rewards for a minimum of care. When in bloom, keep the flowers out of strong light to ensure they last as long as possible.

FLOWER
10cm (4in) wide

FLOWER SPIKE
23cm (9in) long

PLANT SIZE
30cm (12in) high

POT SIZE
12cm (5in)

TEMPERATURE
Cool

Miltoniopsis **Lyceana 'Stampland'**

This lovely two-coloured pansy orchid has the large lip, typical of the genus, which has become the most attractive part of the flower, especially when the central mask is well-defined and of a contrasting colour. *Miltoniopsis* Lyceana is an older hybrid, raised in Britain in 1925 by Charlesworth & Co., a nursery in Haywards Heath, West Sussex, England. 'Stampland' was awarded a first class certificate in 1926, when it became the benchmarkfor future generations.

FLOWER
10cm (4in) wide

FLOWER SPIKE
23cm (9in) long

PLANT SIZE
30cm (12in) high

POT SIZE
12cm (5in)

TEMPERATURE
Cool

Miltoniopsis **Mrs J B Crum 'Chelsea'**

There are many fine red hybrids available, but few are as rich of this outstanding variety, raised in 1931. The whole flower has a velvety appearance, enhanced by the white margin around the lip. Water can spoil the blooms, so take care when watering these plants. Flowers produced during the main spring flowering season will be of a superior quality to those produced later in the autumn, though a second flowering is always welcome.

FLOWER
10cm (4in) wide

FLOWER SPIKE
23cm (9in) long

PLANT SIZE
30cm (12in) high

POT SIZE
12cm (5in) high

TEMPERATURE
Cool

Miltoniopsis **Robert Strauss 'White Flag'**

Only a few of the top-quality hybrids have flowers of the purest white, as illustrated here, where the central markings of red and yellow set off the flower. The outstanding quality of 'White Flag' is the roundness of its flamboyant lip, in perfect balance with the size of the petals and sepals. The adult plant carries 4-6 large blooms on a spike and a well-grown plant usually produces two flower spikes from the pseudobulb at the same time.

FLOWER
10cm (4in) wide

FLOWER SPIKE
23cm (9in) long

PLANT SIZE
30cm (12in) high

POT SIZE
12cm (5in)

TEMPERATURE
Cool

Miltoniopsis **St Helier 'Pink Delight'**

This charming form of St Helier is an example of the variation to be found in the Jersey-raised hybrids. It produces high-quality, long-lasting blooms at their best in spring, offering a combination of light, veined pink on the lip, dominated by the dark red butterfly-shaped mask at the centre; a broad white border separates the colours. This beautifully balanced flower was raised in Jersey by the Eric Young Orchid Foundation, leaders in hybridizing this genus since the 1970s.

FLOWER
10cm (4in) wide

FLOWER SPIKE
23cm (9in) long

PLANT SIZE
30cm (12in) high

POT SIZE
12cm (5in)

TEMPERATURE
Cool

Miltoniopsis **Zoro x Saffron Surprise**

In this yellow flower of exceptional quality, a deep red-brown mask is combined with the two 'thumbprints' on the petals. Yellow hybrids are hard to produce because yellow is not a prominent colour among the species, and many tone down to cream soon after opening. Allow orchids like this to grow on to a specimen size, without dividing, for a number of years. A large plant with several pseudobulbs flowering at once gives an impressive display and extends the period of bloom, as not all flowers open at the same time.

FLOWER
10cm (4in) wide

FLOWER SPIKE
23cm (9in) long

PLANT SIZE
30cm (12in) high

POT SIZE
12cm (5in)

TEMPERATURE
Cool

Miltoniopsis **Nancy Binks**

The lip of this lovely hybrid, raised by an amateur grower, Dr Jim Binks, in 1985, shows an outstanding pattern. It resembles a velvet cushion, at the centre of the flower, while the cherry red on the petals contrasts with the white background. Allow the flower spikes to assume their natural arching habit, which is the best way to show off the blooms.

FLOWER
10cm (4in) wide

FLOWER SPIKE
23cm (9in) long

PLANT SIZE
30cm (12in) high

POT SIZE
12cm (5in)

TEMPERATURE
Cool

Miltoniopsis vexillaria **'Josephina'**

Since 1872, when it was brought into cultivation, *Miltoniopsis vexillaria* was known as 'the scarlet odontoglossum'. The species is unique in its soft pastel colouring and its large, flat flowers on gently pendent sprays. It blooms in early summer, when its fragrant flowers last up to 3 weeks. Today this is something of a collector's plant, prized for its natural beauty and maintained in specialist nurseries where it is still used for breeding.

FLOWER
10cm (4in) wide

FLOWER SPIKE
23cm (9in) long

PLANT SIZE
30cm (12in) high

POT SIZE
10cm (4in)

TEMPERATURE
Cool

Miltonia spectabilis

Closely related to the colourful *Miltoniopsis* are the miltonias. The flowers are generally smaller and less flamboyant, but the resemblance is clear in the dominant lip with attractive markings, seen in this species introduced from Brazil in 1837. Miltonias also produce only a single bloom on a stem and they lack the fragrance of *Miltoniopsis*. Although closely related, these two genera will, surprisingly, not breed together.

FLOWER
10cm (4in) wide

FLOWER SPIKE
10cm (4in) long

PLANT SIZE
15cm (6in) high

POT SIZE
10cm (4in)

TEMPERATURE
Cool

Miltonia clowesii

Miltonia clowesii is a species from Central America belonging to a small genus once included in *Odontoglossum*, but now separated from it. It has the typical star-shaped flowers, with erect and pointed lateral petals and fiddle-shaped lip. Spaced well apart on a tall, upright spike, they are richly coloured, waxy and fragrant. The main flowering season is summer and autumn. The plant produces modest-sized pseudobulbs with slender mid-green leaves.

FLOWER
5cm (2in) wide

FLOWER SPIKE
60cm (24in) long

PLANT SIZE
30cm (12in) high

POT SIZE
10cm (4in)

TEMPERATURE
Cool

Slipper

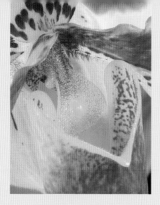

Slipper orchids – *Paphiopedilum* and *Phragmipedium* – are a fascinating and diverse group, having separated from the rest of the orchid family and developed their own plant and flower structure. Their distinct trade mark, the pouch or slipper, is a further modification of the third petal or lip. Today all slipper orchids growing in the wild are endangered species, so their wild collection is banned and no species can be imported or exported without a licence. Tropical paphiopedilums produce two or more thick, fleshy leaves, often mottled; the flower bud emerges from the centre. The more vigorous phragmipediums have long, strap-like leaves and tall, sequential-blooming flower spikes. Both need a warm, well-shaded position, with a minimum night-time temperature of 18°C (64°F).

orchids

Phragmipedium besseae

Until this species was discovered in the 1980s, red was unknown in the genus. It has been responsible for opening up a new line of vibrant red and orange hybrids which are free flowering and easy to grow. The late discovery was partly due to its habit of growing on inaccessible rock faces high in the Andes in Ecuador and Peru. The plant produces tufted growths along a creeping rhizome and blooms mainly in autumn, producing small flowers in succession on a long spike.

FLOWER
8cm (3in) wide

FLOWER SPIKE
30cm (12in) long

PLANT SIZE
25cm (10in) high

POT SIZE
15cm (6in)

TEMPERATURE
Intermediate

Phragmipedium **Grouville**

This is a light pink variation among mainly red-flowered hybrids. The flowers exhibit the familiar classic shape but with pastel rather than rich red hues. A generation on from P. Eric Young (see page 114), the flower shape reflects the continuing influence of *P. besseae* (see page 106) which imparts red colouring to its hybrids. With further buds extending the flower spike, the plant remains in flower for months before the last flower drops.

FLOWER
8cm (3in) wide

FLOWER SPIKE
30cm (12in) long

PLANT SIZE
30cm (12in) high

POT SIZE
15cm (6in)

TEMPERATURE
Intermediate

Phragmipedium longifolium

The dramatic flowers of this wonderful display species, with their long, narrow, drooping petals, illustrate why phragmipediums are called mandarin orchids. Close inspection of the greenish flowers reveals minute spotting and light striping through petals and pouch while the staminode at the centre is distinguished by a short fringe of black hairs. It has tall, lush foliage and the extremely long spikes produce many flowers in succession.

FLOWER
12cm (5in) wide

FLOWER SPIKE
2m (6ft) long

PLANT SIZE
60cm (24in) high

POT SIZE
20cm (8in)

TEMPERATURE
Intermediate

Phragmipedium **Beauport**

This hybrid was raised in 1997 at the Eric Young Orchid Foundation in the Channel Islands. Rounded petals and an egg-shaped pouch set it apart, combined with its deep, rosy red colouring. The flowers are produced in succession on an extending upright flower spike which may not require tying. The plant blooms in late spring from the previous season's growth.

FLOWER
8cm (3in) wide

FLOWER SPIKE
30cm (12in) long

PLANT SIZE
20cm (8in) high

POT SIZE
15cm (6in)

TEMPERATURE
Intermediate

Phragmipedium **Eric Young**

This distinctively shaped flower glows
with warm orange tones, while its long,
semi-drooping petals sweep down from
the horizontal, half-encircling the pouch.
A small dorsal sepal is another feature.
Raised in 1991, this is one of the finest
new hybrids achieved through the
introduction of the magnificent *P. besseae*,
which imparts its unique red colour to
its progeny; the other parent is
P. longifolium (see page 110). The large
flowers are not heavily textured and are
easily supported on the upright spike.

FLOWER 12cm (5in) wide
FLOWER SPIKE 45cm (18in) long
PLANT SIZE 30cm (12in) high
POT SIZE 15cm (6in)
TEMPERATURE Intermediate

Phragmipedium **Sedenii**

This beautiful hybrid was raised in 1873 by Veitch & Sons. It has stood the test of time and is still available today, but only as a rare collectors' item. From one of its parents it has inherited the light pastel colouring typical of older hybrids and in direct contrast to the bright colours of modern phragmipediums. The tall flower spike carries several buds, not all of which will open simultaneously.

FLOWER
6cm (2½in) wide

FLOWER SPIKE
45cm (18in) long

PLANT SIZE
30cm (12in) high

POT SIZE
15cm (6in) high

TEMPERATURE
Intermediate

Phragmipedium **Don Wimber**

In this exciting, richly coloured modern hybrid the flower is distinctly triangular in shape, complemented by a well-balanced pouch. The blooms appear on a tall spike, which produces further buds from the apex as it extends. The plant is a strong, robust grower with long, strap-like leaves. These orchids like to be kept well watered all year so their fleshy leaves do not become dehydrated or limp. Light spraying is beneficial.

FLOWER 10cm (4in) wide
FLOWER SPIKE 60cm (24in) long
PLANT SIZE 45cm (18in) high
POT SIZE 20cm (8in) high
TEMPERATURE Intermediate

Phragmipedium **St Peter**

The 'Saints' series all come from the Eric Young Orchid Foundation in the Channel Islands, whose fame has spread worldwide. St Peter is a further variation on the theme of red-flowered hybrids. The flower spikes are tall and gracious and need plenty of headroom if they are to be grown well. This long-petalled hybrid carries a more open pouch, which is a distinctive feature of the flower.

FLOWER 12cm (5in) wide
FLOWER SPIKE 45cm (18in) long
PLANT SIZE 30cm (12in) high
POT SIZE 20cm (8in)
TEMPERATURE Intermediate

Paphiopedilum **Chiquita**

This is an example of the new breed
of paphiopedilum, using *P. primulinum* to
bring in a different colour range. This
lime-yellow species, found in 1972 in
Sumatra, belongs to a small group of
related species with narrow, wavy-edged
petals and a distinctive pouch. The light,
open flower shape is a contrast to
the heavy, rounded blooms usually seen
within the genus. Several flowers are
produced at the end of the spike but only
one opens at a time.

FLOWER
8cm (3in) wide

FLOWER SPIKE
25cm (10in) long

PLANT SIZE
20cm (8in) high

POT SIZE
10cm (4in)

TEMPERATURE
Intermediate

Paphiopedilum **Holdenii**

FLOWER
10cm (4in) wide

FLOWER SPIKE
25cm (10in) long

PLANT SIZE
12cm (5in) high

POT SIZE
10cm (4in)

TEMPERATURE
Intermediate

There are a number of these clean, clear, green-flowered types among the mottled-leaf paphiopedilums. The dorsal sepal carries the typical 'humbug' stripes while the rest of the flower is self-coloured. The attractive light green mottled foliage is compact, with oval leaves. A single bloom, produced on a tall stem, needs a thin cane to hold it upright. Wait until the flower has opened and become set, then tie it back to the cane so it can be seen front-facing.

Paphiopedilum **Silverlight**

This smaller-flowered orchid exhibits the butter-yellow colouring of *P. primulinum*, the species from which it was raised. This group of sequential-flowering hybrids prefer a warmer environment, reflecting the original home of the dominant parent, a low-altitude species from Sumatra. The slender foliage is mid- to light green, indicating a preference for shady conditions. Apart from yellow, light green and white are seen in this new line of breeding.

FLOWER
8cm (3in) wide

FLOWER SPIKE
15cm (6in) long

PLANT SIZE
12cm (5in) high

POT SIZE
10cm (4in)

TEMPERATURE
Intermediate

Paphiopedilum **Gina Short**

Pink-flowered pahiopedilums have always been unusual but are much admired. Pink was unknown in the genus until the accidental discovery of *P. delenatii* in 1913 by a French soldier fighting in Indochina (now Vietnam). The large flowers have an egg-shaped pouch and 1-3 summer-blooming flowers can be produced on a single short spike. These compact plants also produce exquisite foliage, darkly tessellated on the surface with purple peppering on the undersides.

FLOWER
5cm (2in) wide

FLOWER SPIKE
25cm (10in) long

PLANT SIZE
10cm (4in) high

POT SIZE
10cm (4in)

TEMPERATURE
Intermediate

Paphiopedilum villosum

This cool-growing Himalayan species was discovered in 1853, growing on trees in the wet, mountainous areas of Burma at an altitude of 2,000m (6,000ft), where the nights are cool. It has slender, dark green foliage and carries single flowers in late autumn and winter; the colour of polished brass, it has a high gloss to its waxy petals and pouch. This species was used to produce many of today's fine hybrids, but is now less widely grown as the stock of cultivated plants dwindle and it is no longer available from the wild.

FLOWER
10cm (4in) wide

FLOWER SPIKE
15cm (6in) long

PLANT SIZE
25cm (10in) high

POT SIZE
10cm (4in)

TEMPERATURE
Cool

Paphiopedilum Deperle

This is a popular hybrid between
the Vietnam species *P. delenatii* and the
more recently discovered Sumatran
species, *P. primulinum*. The latter,
described in 1973, has opened up a new
breeding line for small yellow-flowered
hybrids and has proved the dominant
parent in this 1980 French-bred plant.
The compact blooms, opening one at a
time in spring, resemble those of
P. primulinum in shape. Their colour, a
buttery yellow, belies the other parent,
which often passes on its pink pigment.

FLOWER
6cm (2½in) wide

FLOWER SPIKE
25cm (10in) long

PLANT SIZE
15cm (6in) high

POT SIZE
10cm (4in)

TEMPERATURE
Intermediate

Paphiopedilum **Pinocchio**

Raised in France in 1977, the flower of P. Pinocchio is probably the smallest in the genus. It has pretty, compact blooms borne on a long flower spike, and the centre of the bloom shows a deep green rostellum, or column. While these orchids do not eat or digest insects, they do trap them when they slip and fall into the pouch. The insect can easily escape, but in doing so either removes or deposits its pollen.

FLOWER
8cm (3in) wide

FLOWER SPIKE
25cm (10in) long

PLANT SIZE
15cm (6in) high

POT SIZE
10cm (4in)

TEMPERATURE
Intermediate

Paphiopedilum **Jersey Freckles**

This handsome hybrid is typical of a multitude of similar hybrids which have both cool- and warmer-growing parents in their background. Jersey Freckles is a green-leafed type which may be grown in a warm and shady position indoors or in a heated greenhouse. These plants dislike too much direct light and prefer a shady place where the sun does not reach. A single flower, lasting up to 8 weeks, blooms inwinter; large specimens produce more than one flower on separate stems from each new growth.

FLOWER
12cm (5in) wide

FLOWER SPIKE
20cm (8in) long

PLANT SIZE
12cm (5in) high

POT SIZE
10cm (4in)

TEMPERATURE
Intermediate

Paphiopedilum **Jac Flash**

This is one of the modern breed of dark-coloured hybrids, a programme which has led to some exciting shades very near to the elusive black. A large, flared dorsal sepal is heavily stained purple, with darker veining, while the swept-down petals are green and purple, and the pouch shows the darkest colour of all. The compact plants also produce mottled foliage, with rounded leaves, and make good houseplants even when not in bloom. It blooms in summer, lasting for weeks.

FLOWER
5cm (2in) wide

FLOWER SPIKE
25cm (10in) long

PLANT SIZE
10cm (4in) high

POT SIZE
10cm (4in)

TEMPERATURE
Intermediate

Paphiopedilum **Prime Child**

This unusual-looking hybrid has been raised from the Borneo species *P. rothschildianum*, noted for its extraordinary long, narrow petals. The downward-swooping petals of P. Prime Child are spotted along their length. While the species produces multi-flowering spikes, this hybrid flowers in succession like its other parent, *P. primulinum*, with one bud opening at a time. The hybrid, raised in California in 1985, is now quite widely available.

FLOWER 18cm (7in) wide
FLOWER SPIKE 30cm (12in) long
PLANT SIZE 20cm (8in) high
POT SIZE 10cm (4in)
TEMPERATURE Intermediate

Epiden

drums

Epidendrum means 'upon a tree' and refers to the orchids' epiphytic habit of attaching themselves to trees as an anchor for growth. This is a genus of mainly tall-growing orchids with slender, reed-like canes and foliage; a smaller group produce tall, slim pseudobulbs with a pair of rigid long, oval leaves. The small flowers come from the top of the stem, blooming for months. As the plants grow they make copious aerial roots and self-propagate from the apex of old stems – these can be potted up. Water and spray regularly, applying feed every third watering.

Epidendrum ciliare

Originating in the West Indies and tropical America, this white *Epidendrum* is one of a group which produce slender pseudobulbs with a single leaf. Described in 1759, it is one of the earliest-known tropical orchids. Up to 8 flowers are produced on a lengthy stem from the top of the pseudobulb. They have long, narrow petals and sepals, with a deeply lobed lip, frilled at the edge. The autumn-blooming species can be shy to flower if given insufficient light at the end of summer when the pseudobulbs mature.

FLOWER
9cm (3½in) wide

PLANT SIZE
30cm (12in) high

POT SIZE
15cm (6in)

TEMPERATURE
Intermediate

Epidendrum **Plastic Doll**

Looking at the flower shape and coloration of this unusual hybrid, it becomes obvious that one parent is the bright E. *pseudepidendrum* (see page 154). E. Plastic Doll blooms over a long period in summer, after which it rests and needs less water. Leaves are shed a few at a time from the older canes, which eventually become leafless before shrivelling and dying. The tall plants do best in small pots but need a supporting cane.

FLOWER
5cm (2in) wide

PLANT SIZE
30-100cm
(12-40in) high

POT SIZE
15cm (6in)

TEMPERATURE
Intermediate

Epidendrum ilense

This tall, robust species from Central America produces leafy stems that bloom from the apex when growth is complete. The extraordinary flowers are carried on a slender, arching stem and appear in succession over a long period, with 3-4 blooms out at a time. The lip is bulbous at the centre, its edge deeply frilled to give a bearded effect. Leafless old stems continue to bloom over several years. This unusual plant needs a large container to stop it getting top-heavy.

FLOWER
5cm (2in) wide

PLANT SIZE
30-100cm
(12-40in) high

POT SIZE
15cm (6in)

TEMPERATURE
Intermediate

Epidendrum pseudepidendrum

The epidendrums are a genus of tall-growing plants with thin, leafy canes or with slender, one-leafed pseudobulbs. This species belongs to the reed-type epidendrums as the former group is known. It comes from Costa Rica where it grows on trees, producing extensive stems that bloom from the apex. Several flowers appear on an arching stem with narrow, bright green sepals and petals; the orange lip is glossy, waxy and almost plastic in appearance.

FLOWER
5cm (2in) wide

PLANT SIZE
30-100cm
(12-40in) high

POT SIZE
18cm (7in)

TEMPERATURE
Intermediate

Pleio

nes

This small genus of modest-growing orchids develop round pseudobulbs with a single leaf, shed in autumn, after which they need a cold, dry rest in winter. Pleiones prefer being crowded and several are usually grown in a shallow pan, in a soilless compost of peat substitute and grit, to give a glorious show in early spring. Repot annually, before flowering, cutting off the oldest pseudobulbs and dead roots; keep evenly watered in summer, feeding lightly every third watering. Maintain a minimum winter night temperature of 5-7°C (40-45°F) and a daytime summer maximum of 24°C (75°F).

Pleione **Shantung 'Ridgeway'**

This beautiful apricot-coloured hybrid, produced in 1977, is the result of crossing a pink form of the well-known species P. *formosana* with the lesser-known P. *confusa*, the only yellow species in the genus. Originally known as P. *forrestii*, this latter species was collected in south-west China in 1904 by the plant collector George Forrest.

FLOWER
8cm (3in) wide

FLOWER SPIKE
15-20cm (4-6in) long

PLANT SIZE
15cm (6in) high

PAN SIZE
10cm (4in)

TEMPERATURE
Cool

Pleione **Tongariro**

This hybrid, which shows a strong resemblance to the original species, is a cross between *P.* Versailles (see page 167) and *P. speciosa* (see page 163). Although *P.* Versailles itself was raised in France, almost all the later hybrids have been produced in Britain by Ian Butterfield, a nurseryman who specializes in this genus; many carry the names of well-known volcanoes.

FLOWER
6cm (2½in) wide

FLOWER SPIKE
10-15cm (4-6in) long

PLANT SIZE
12cm (5in) high

PAN SIZE
10cm (4in)

TEMPERATURE
Cool

Pleione speciosa

This bright magenta species, in cultivation since 1914, is undoubtedly one of the richest-coloured in this much-loved genus of small plants. *P. speciosa* is typical of the genus with its widespread petals and sepals and generously coloured lip, gaily patterned with yellow striations and red dots. A single flower is usually produced but occasionally two will open on the stem; the blooms last for about 10 days.

FLOWER 6cm (2½in) wide
FLOWER SPIKE 10-15cm (4-6in) long
PLANT SIZE 12cm (5in) high
PAN SIZE 10cm (4in)
TEMPERATURE Cool

Pleione formosana var. semi-alba

This is probably the best known of the species and among the easiest to grow. Because *P. formosana* is very variable, with many colour variations, selective breeding has enabled a wide range of colours to be produced among its hybrids. This pleione has glistening white sepals and petals, with discreet yellow and brown lip colouring. A pure white is also found, devoid of colouring on the lip. It is not unusual for two flowers to be produced on a stem.

FLOWER
6cm (2½in) wide

FLOWER SPIKE
10-15cm
(4-6in) long

PLANT SIZE
12cm (5in) high

PAN SIZE
10cm (4in)

TEMPERATURE
Cool

Pleione **Versailles**

Versailles was the first hybrid to be
produced in this genus and, since
1963, when it first flowered, numerous
further spring-flowering hybrids have
been made, raising the profile of this
attractive genus. The narrow, oval
petals and sepals have a glistening,
soft texture and the large, frilled lip is
delicately coloured at the centre, with
streaks or spots of a different colour.

FLOWER 5cm (2in) wide
PLANT SIZE 15cm (6in) high
PAN SIZE 10cm (4in)
TEMPERATURE Cool

Coelogynes

These two charming genera are grouped together because of their similar growth and identical cultural needs. All are compact, evergreen plants with pseudobulbs and a fine rooting system; they flower from early spring through summer. Grow in bark compost in pots or hanging baskets and keep well shaded in summer, increasing the brightness until they are in full light for winter. Water and feed them well in spring and early summer. Provide a minimum temperature of 10°C (50°F) and a maximum of 30°C (85°F).

& Encyclias

Coelogyne **Memoria William Micholitz 'Burnham'**

This wonderfully coloured orchid, with its glistening white petals and sepals and lip of almost solid gold, is an outstanding cross in a genus which has produced very few hybrids of note. It produces a large plant with sturdy, cone-shaped pseudobulbs and a pair of mid-green oval leaves. It blooms during spring and early summer, on a flower spike carrying up to 6 blooms.

FLOWER
9cm (3½in) wide

PLANT SIZE
45cm (18in) high

POT SIZE
18cm (7in)

TEMPERATURE
Cool

Coelogyne ochracea

Coelogyne ochracea is one of the prettiest species in this genus. After resting for a few weeks in winter, new growth extends from the base and the flower spike develops from within the centre of the young growth. In spring the flower spike carries up to a dozen sparkling white fragrant flowers, their lips attractively patterned in orange, yellow and brown.

FLOWER
2.5cm (1in) wide

FLOWER SPIKE
20cm (8in) long

PLANT SIZE
30cm (12in) high

POT SIZE
15cm (6in)

TEMPERATURE
Cool

Coelogyne fuscescens

This dwarf-flowering species makes an ideal windowsill orchid which will never outgrow its position. A native of India and Nepal, it was first described in 1830. The oval pseudobulbs carry two leaves, from between which a single flower is produced, with a prettily marked lip. A large plant will be covered in blooms in autumn. Plants readily divide if space is limited or, if allowed to grow on, form a dense mat of growths to cover the container.

FLOWER 3cm (1¼in) wide
PLANT SIZE 30cm (12in) high
POT SIZE 10cm (4in)
TEMPERATURE Cool

Coelogyne mooreana **'Brockhurst'**

Coelogyne mooreana was discovered in Vietnam in 1906 and named after F. W. Moore of the Glasnevin Botanic Gardens, Dublin. One of the biggest species in the genus, it produces spectacular pristine white blooms with broad sepals and petals; its lip carries a deep yellow stain at the centre. 'Brockhurst' is a handsome, robust plant with cone-shaped pseudobulbs and two narrow light green leaves; do not let the pseudobulbs shrivel.

FLOWER
9cm (3½in) wide

PLANT SIZE
45cm (18in) high

POT SIZE
18cm (7in)

TEMPERATURE
Cool

Coelogyne barbata

This tall species became popular after 1878 when the first living orchid plants were sent from the hills of northern India. It produces egg-shaped pseudobulbs topped by a pair of dark green, narrowly oval leaves between which the flower spikes appear. The large, glistening white flowers have a dark brown bearded lip and a fringe of black hairs. It blooms in winter, with flowers opening in succession along the stem, the first remaining fresh well after the last has opened.

FLOWER
5cm (2in) wide

PLANT SIZE
30cm (12in) high

POT SIZE
15cm (6in)

TEMPERATURE
Cool

Encyclia lancifolia

This pretty, highly fragrant Mexican species is one of several having creamy white flowers with a cockleshell-shaped lip held at the top. The long sepals and petals hang loosely below the lip. The compact plant has short, club-shaped pseudobulbs and a pair of light green leaves; the upright flower spike comes from between the leaves. This is an ideal species for the home grower looking for compact plants with interesting flowers.

FLOWER
2cm (1in) wide

FLOWER SPIKE
15cm (6in) long

PLANT SIZE
18cm (7in) high

POT SIZE
12cm (5in) high

TEMPERATURE
Cool

Encyclia radiata

This is a delightful encyclia to grow. The plant produces slender pseudobulbs with a pair of mid-green leaves; the upright flower spike carries up to a dozen cheery little blooms. These have a strong fragrance, and on a large plant the scent will fill a room. Found in Guatemala, Honduras and Mexico, this plant can be grown on to specimen size as it rarely drops its leaves and looks good for many years without needing to be divided. It blooms in summer.

FLOWER
2cm (1in) wide

FLOWER SPIKE
15cm (6in) long

PLANT SIZE
18cm (7in) high

POT SIZE
12cm (5in)

TEMPERATURE
Cool

Encyclia **Sunburst**

This is an ideal windowsill plant that retains its compact stature and easy flowering. Blooming in summer as the pseudobulbs mature, it needs a rest in winter. This is one of a few hybrids raised from the bright E. *vitellina* (see page 190) and the highly fragrant E. *radiata* (see page 183). The cross, first raised in Hawaii in 1962, produces long-lasting flowers on an upright spike; they open a delicate shade of apricot and tone down to creamy-white.

FLOWER
3cm (1¼in) wide

PLANT SIZE
15cm (6in) high

POT SIZE
10cm (4in)

TEMPERATURE
Cool

Encyclia brassavolae

Among the encyclias is a group carrying spindly flowers on a spike growing from the apex of the pseudobulb; one of the most colourful is E. *brassavolae*. This summer-blooming species has tall, slender pseudobulbs with two narrow oval leaves and the upright spike carries up to a dozen light green flowers; the end of the white oval-shaped lip is tipped rosy mauve. In a pot, the pseudobulbs will quickly fill the surface space; it is better grown in a hanging wooden slatted basket.

FLOWER
4cm (1½in) wide

PLANT SIZE
30cm (12in) high

POT SIZE
15cm (6in)

TEMPERATURE
Cool

Encyclia vitellina

This species is unique in the genus for its bright, vermilion-red flowers. The sepals and petals are oval and equally spaced and the small, duckbill-shaped lip is orange. The flower spike is usually held upright above the plant and carries up to a dozen flowers, blooming in late summer and autumn. The plant originates from Mexico and was first described in 1833.

FLOWER
2cm (1in) wide

PLANT SIZE
15cm (6in) high

POT SIZE
8cm (3in)

TEMPERATURE
Cool

Encyclia cochleata

A large number of encyclias produce
flowers with the lip at the top. This
species is known as the cockleshell orchid,
but also the octopus orchid, alluding
to its long, drooping, ribbon-like petals.
The green and black flowers come from
the top of the club-shaped pseudobulb
in a succession lasting weeks or months.
A great orchid for beginners, it starts
flowering on a very young plant, then
gives unlimited exotic-looking flowers; on
reaching maturity, it blooms perpetually.

FLOWER
3cm (1¼in) wide

PLANT SIZE
30cm (12in) high

POT SIZE
12cm (5in)

TEMPERATURE
Cool

Dendro

This immense genus of colourful orchids has evolved many distinct types. The *Dendrobium nobile*-type hybrids, or 'bamboo orchids', produce tall, jointed pseudobulbs, termed canes. Flower stems produced from the side of the canes each bear two flowers in spring. The fast summer growing period is followed by a winter rest. They benefit from high summer temperatures up to 30°C (85°F) with a night-time minimum of 10°C (50°F) in winter. *Phalaenopsis*-type dendrobiums produce elongated pseudobulbs (canes) and bloom from the top half of the leading cane. They need light combined with warmth (a winter minimum of 13°C/55°F) and humidity.

biums

Dendrobium **All-Seasons Blue**

D. All Seasons Blue, raised in Thailand
in 1995, is one of many hybrids bred
from the Australian species of hard-
caned dendrobiums. Their more rigid
canes remain upright without staking,
their flowers produced on spikes from a
terminal node in autumn. The equally-
proportioned sepals and petals are
spread wide, while the lip is small and
neat, of similar plain colouring.

FLOWER
4cm (1½in) wide

PLANT SIZE
30cm (12in) high

POT SIZE
15cm (6in)

TEMPERATURE
Intermediate

Dendrobium **Dale Takiguchi**

This attractive *Phalaenopsis*-type hybrid illustrates the beauty of the clear, pale-coloured flowers which can be produced by breeding from white, or albino, forms of the species. This is one of the hard-caned dendrobiums whose tall canes, pointed at the top, can remain evergreen for 2-3 years. Oval leaves cover the top half of the canes only. The plant blooms freely in spring and summer, producing its lovely flowers on arching sprays, which last several weeks in perfection.

FLOWER 6cm (2½in) wide
PLANT SIZE 40cm (16in) high
POT SIZE 15cm (6in)
TEMPERATURE Intermediate

Dendrobium miyaki

This pretty Philippines species produces long, pendant canes leafed along their length. Rosy-mauve flowers, produced from side nodes along the canes, appear in a drooping cluster in spring, following a dry winter rest. In summer, it likes to be sprayed and kept moist while the canes develop; good light is another factor in ensuring a show of flowers. It blooms and re-blooms from the older, leafless canes, when these have matured. Best grown in a hanging basket, close to a window.

FLOWER
1cm (½in) wide

PLANT SIZE
30cm (12in) high

POT SIZE
10cm (4in)

TEMPERATURE
Intermediate

Dendrobium **Oriental Paradise**

One of the *Dendrobium nobile*-type group, this hybrid exhibits large, rounded flowers with a circular lip of equal proportions. The range of colour among pinks, mauves, yellows and white is almost endless, each hybrid possessing its own unique lip coloration and central highlight. Because of the infinite variations in colour, it is best to look for these plants in flower in spring to ensure that you select the colouring you like best.

FLOWER
6cm (2½in) wide

PLANT SIZE
45cm (18in) high

POT SIZE
15cm (6in)

TEMPERATURE
Cool

Dendrobium **Tokunaga**

This is an unusual hybrid raised from a distinctive New Guinea species. The small-growing plant produces club-shaped pseudobulbs with leathery terminal leaves. The extraordinary blooms, whitish with light spotting on the outside of the petals, sport a small, neat, light green lip. Up to 6 flowers, carried on a loose spike, will last for 6 months. *D. atroviolaceum*, dominant in this cross, is very fragrant.

FLOWER 3cm (1¼in) wide
PLANT SIZE 30cm (12in) high
POT SIZE 10cm (4in)
TEMPERATURE Intermediate

Dendrobium senile

In this pretty dwarf species from Thailand the canes are covered in dense white hairs, forming a protective layer. The waxy flowers, produced in ones and twos on a short stem from the leaf axils, are fragrant and last for several weeks in spring. They are bright yellow with a green centre to the lip. Leaves are usually shed after a year or two and the plant can become completely leafless during the winter rest, when it needs to be be in full light and kept dry.

FLOWER
2.5cm (1in) wide

PLANT SIZE
10cm (4in) high

POT SIZE
8cm (3in)

TEMPERATURE
Intermediate

Dendrobium **Prima Donna**

D. Prima Donna is a *Dendrobium nobile*-type hybrid with regal blooms. The Indian species has had a dramatic effect on the flowers raised from it, which are well-rounded in shape and heightened in colouring. Buds appear in early spring along the length of the mature canes. Commence watering as they develop, which will happen at the same time as the new growths are initiated to start the new growing season.

FLOWER
8cm (3in) wide

PLANT SIZE
45cm (18in) high

POT SIZE
15cm (6in)

TEMPERATURE
Cool

Dendrobium **Superstar Champion**

This is a modern-day *D. nobile* type of hybrid. Its canes are stout and shortened rather than long and thin as in most species. Plants grow well during the summer, making up their canes in a few months, then rest in winter, needing little or no watering; water only if the canes shrivel. In spring there will be an explosion of buds along the the newest cane, and the flowers will cover the plant. Colours can vary from white through yellow and pink to deep shades of mauve-red, with contrasting lip decorations.

FLOWER
6cm (2½in) wide

PLANT SIZE
45cm (18in) high

POT SIZE
15cm (6in)

TEMPERATURE
Cool

Dendrobium infundibulum

This beautiful species from Burma produces a handsome plant with tall canes densely covered in fine black hairs. The flowers appear in threes or fours on stems opposite each leaf axil along the length of the cane, each large bloom a delicate papery white with a golden yellow centre to the lip. It is one of the easiest dendrobiums to grow and flower to perfection, provided it is given plenty of water and light, moist conditions in the summer growing months.

FLOWER 10cm (4in) wide
PLANT SIZE 45cm (18in) high
POT SIZE 12cm (5in)
TEMPERATURE Cool

Dendrobium **Tancho Queen**

This a *D. nobile*-type hybrid producing the typical 'canes', jointed along their length. This group flowers on the younger canes while still in leaf. One of the lighter coloured hybrids, the beautifully rounded blooms of *D.* Tancho Queen contrast clear white petals and sepals with an almost black disc in the middle of the large, frilled lip.

FLOWER
6cm (2½in) wide

PLANT SIZE
45cm (18in) high

POT SIZE
15cm (6in)

TEMPERATURE
Cool

Dendrobium **Thongchai Gold**

D. Thongchai Gold is one of a number of hybrids raised in Thailand which have yellow-gold flowers, the dark red-mauve lip making a stunning contrast. The petals, narrow at the base, are rounded out at their tips, while the smaller sepals are often lighter in colour. The enduring flowers are carried on spikes produced from the top half of the canes.

FLOWER
5cm (2in) wide

PLANT SIZE
30cm (12in) high

POT SIZE
12cm (5in)

TEMPERATURE
Intermediate

Dendrobium nobile var. cooksonii

In this colourful variety of *D. nobile*, the flower exhibits the rose-pink colouring of the type but also carries a replica pattern of the lip marking on the lateral petals. It is capable of flowering the entire length of its newest canes, but flowering to such perfection takes skill. In winter the plant needs a dry rest; if watering is started too early in the year, before the flower buds are fully developed, they will turn into adventitious growths instead of flowers.

FLOWER
5cm (2in) wide

PLANT SIZE
45cm (18in) high

POT SIZE
15cm (6in)

TEMPERATURE
Cool

Dendrobium nobile var. virginale

This pure white Indian species has been in cultivation for 200 years. It produces tall, leafy canes which become deciduous after 2-3 years. The flowers are carried on short stems in ones and twos along the length of the newest cane. One of the naturally occurring varieties within the species is this lovely albino form which lacks the usual rose-pink colour. To stop them becoming top-heavy, place the pot inside another, larger pot with stones at the bottom. The plant blooms in spring and will last for 3 weeks.

FLOWER
5cm (2in) wide

PLANT SIZE
45cm (18in) high

POT SIZE
15cm (6in)

TEMPERATURE
Cool

Dendrobium victoria-regina

FLOWER
2cm (1in) wide

PLANT SIZE
30cm (12in) high

POT SIZE
10cm (4in)

TEMPERATURE
Cool

This species produces slender canes that are deciduous after 2-3 years. As the canes mature they assume a pendant position so are best cultivated in small pots or baskets where their natural habit can develop. Alternatively, tie the canes into an upright position, which does not affect the plant's flowering. The small mauve flowers are produced in clusters of two or three from midway to the top of the canes; several canes can flower in one season. Good light is needed at all times of year.

Cattleya

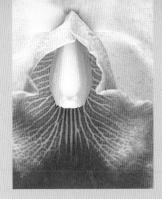

Behind this alliance lies a web of interwoven hybrids, centered around cattleyas and laelias. Evergreen cattleyas produce short or tall club-shaped pseudobulbs, supporting one leaf or two. The rigid leaves are thick and leathery and the fragrant blooms, up to 12cm (5in) across, are fabulous. Most species are autumn- or spring-flowering. The laelias are similar, with elongated pseudobulbs and a single oval leaf. Select compact forms for indoor use and give as much filtered light as possible. All need a minimum temperature of 13°C (55°F) on winter nights, with a summer maximum of 30°C (85°F).

alliance

Cattleya **Little Miss Charming**

One of the first tropical orchids to come
into cultivation, cattleyas were highly
prized for their large blooms. The best
are found in the steamy rainforests
of Brazil. In this hybrid the flower is
unusually spaced out, the narrow
petals and sepals neither touching nor
overlapping as in the rounder flowers.
Two or three blooms are produced
on a long stem, while the tall, slender
pseudobulbs have a long, oval leaf.

FLOWER
10cm (4in) wide

PLANT SIZE
30cm (12in) high

POT SIZE
15cm (6in)

TEMPERATURE
Intermediate

Cattleya **Hawaiian Wedding Song**

In this American-raised white hybrid, which is pure *Cattleya*, the petals have become so frilled and enlarged that their shape is almost undefined, causing the flower to lose some of the roundness that is the hallmark of these lovely hybrids. The lip is well defined, however, and exhibits a perfectly frilled edge and deep yellow throat. This modern hybrid is from the 'unifoliate' group, producing one leathery oval leaf.

FLOWER
12cm (5in) wide

PLANT SIZE
38cm (15in) high

POT SIZE
15cm (6in)

TEMPERATURE
Intermediate

Cattleya **Sir Jeremiah Coleman**

In the search for the elusive blue in cattleyas, this plant is supreme. It was raised in the USA in 1976 and named in honour of an eminent breeder of blue-flowered *Cattleya* hybrids of the early twentieth century. It has proved to be a fine breeder of blue cattleyas over the years. Its sepals and petals are eggshell blue, the frilled lip mauve around the edge and yellow-centred. A neat grower, its slender pseudobulbs have a pair of narrow, oval leaves at the apex.

FLOWER
10cm (4in) wide

PLANT SIZE
30cm (12in) high

POT SIZE
15cm (6in)

TEMPERATURE
Intermediate

Laeliocattleya **Veldorado 'Polka'**

The diversity of flower colour in this bigeneric hybrid genus between *Laelia* and *Cattleya* is well illustrated in this superb modern French-bred hybrid. One to three fragrant flowers are produced on the spike, the rich yellow petals and sepals contrasting vividly with the deep ruby lip, shot through with gold veining towards the throat. The plant blooms when the season's pseudobulb is completed, usually autumn. To prolong flowering, place out of strong light while in bloom and keep on the dry side.

FLOWER
12cm (5in) wide

PLANT SIZE
38cm (15in) high

POT SIZE
15cm (6in)

TEMPERATURE
Intermediate

Laeliocattleya **Drumbeat**

The first combination of *Laelia* and *Cattleya* was made in 1887. Many such crosses have been made since, producing fine, large-flowered varieties that display lush colouring on showy blooms which may be white, yellow or shades of lavender-pink or purple. Some are spring- and others autumn-blooming; hybrids take their flowering cue from one parent or the other. *Lc.* Drumbeat has a delightful scent and well-rounded, frilled blooms.

FLOWER
15cm (6in) wide

PLANT SIZE
38cm (15in) high

POT SIZE
15cm (6in)

TEMPERATURE
Intermediate

Laeliocattleya **Elizabeth Fulton 'La Tuilerie'**

Raised in 1977 in the USA, this richly coloured orchid is the result of generations of selective breeding. The coppery colour, rare among cattleyas, is a welcome addition to an already extensive colour range. The sepals and petals display the ideal shape of the genus and the self-coloured lip is a perfect complement. The plant is a neat grower; its slender pseudobulbs carry a single leaf, with the blooms appearing well above the foliage. One to three flowers, usually two, appear in autumn.

FLOWER
12cm (5in) wide

PLANT SIZE
38cm (15in) high

POT SIZE
15cm (6in)

TEMPERATURE
Intermediate

Laeliocattleya **Persepolis**

Laeliocattleya Persepolis is a bigeneric hybrid combining the qualities of *Cattleya* and *Laelia* to produce an outstanding flower with the full *Cattleya* shape and attractive, delicate colouring on the petals and sepals. The lip too, with its magenta colouring, shows a marked *Cattleya* influence. This is an important breeding plant which has gone on to produce mainly summer-blooming white-flowered hybrids. The plant is strong and robust with a thick, leathery leaf. In winter these orchids like

FLOWER
15cm (6in) wide

PLANT SIZE
38cm (15in) high

POT SIZE
15cm (6in)

TEMPERATURE
Intermediate

all the light available, but early spring
sunshine can burn through their tender
leaf structures, so they should be given
some shade, or moved to a shadier
place, from spring onwards, once the
sun starts to gain power.

Epicattleya **Siam Jade**

Epidendrums, syn. encyclias (see pages 146-155) are closely related to cattleyas and help to make up the *Cattleya* alliance. When selected epidendrums are crossed with cattleyas some startlingly different coloured plants emerge, as in this beautiful clear green hybrid. The sepals and petals are thicker-textured than those of other cattleyas, while the lovely cream lip is almost rigid. The compact plant has shortened pseudobulbs; its flowering season varies but it usually blooms in spring.

FLOWER
5cm (2in) wide

PLANT SIZE
10cm (4in) high

POT SIZE
10cm (4in)

TEMPERATURE
Intermediate

Epicattleya **El Hatillo 'Santa Maria'**

This neat-growing orchid combines the qualities of two genera. The *Encyclia* (*Epidendrum*) proves the dominant parent, influencing the flower shape, while the vivid lip colour is typical *Cattleya*. The plant has slender, elongated pseudobulbs supporting a pair of rigid narrow leaves from between which the upright flower spike emerges. This carries 4-5 fragrant flowers, light creamy green with a contrasting lip. The plant likes to be warm and provided with good light all year.

FLOWER
5cm (2in) wide

PLANT SIZE
10cm (4in) high

POT SIZE
12cm (5in)

TEMPERATURE
Intermediate

Phalae

nopsis

For ease of growth and regular flowering, *Phalaenopsis* have no equal. Moth orchids grow from a central rhizome, producing fleshy oval leaves. Modern hybrids do not have a particular season but produce a flower spike in response to the completion of a new leaf. The flowers last for weeks in perfection after which the flower spike can be cut back to a lower node to inititate a secondary flower spike. They prefer semi-shade in a warm area where temperatures fluctuate little between day and night, summer and winter, with a minimum of 18°C (64°F).

Phalaenopsis **Paifang's Golden Lion**

Heavy leopard spotting overlies a
lighter-based flower, giving the impression
of deep rosy-purple. The lateral petals
divide along the centre vein, below
which the colour is intensified. Such
exquisite colouring is found only in this
type of hybrid which produces glossy,
waxy-textured flowers on a short flower
spike. The individual flowers, produced
in succession, bloom for a long time.
As mature flowers fade, new buds open
along an extending stem.

FLOWER
8cm (3in) wide

FLOWER SPIKE
23cm (9in) long

PLANT SIZE
20cm (8in) high

POT SIZE
12cm (5in)

TEMPERATURE
Warm

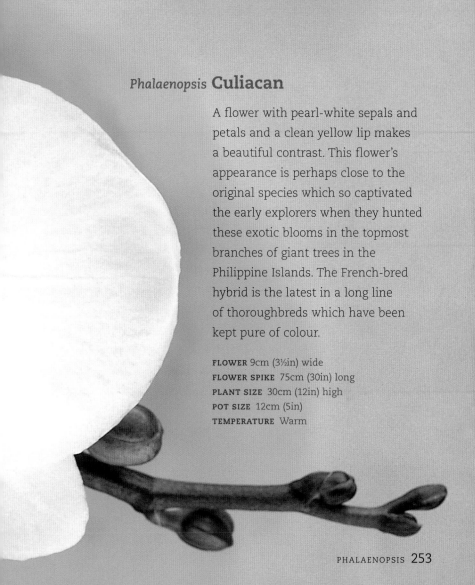

Phalaenopsis **Culiacan**

A flower with pearl-white sepals and petals and a clean yellow lip makes a beautiful contrast. This flower's appearance is perhaps close to the original species which so captivated the early explorers when they hunted these exotic blooms in the topmost branches of giant trees in the Philippine Islands. The French-bred hybrid is the latest in a long line of thoroughbreds which have been kept pure of colour.

FLOWER 9cm (3½in) wide
FLOWER SPIKE 75cm (30in) long
PLANT SIZE 30cm (12in) high
POT SIZE 12cm (5in)
TEMPERATURE Warm

Phalaenopsis **Little Skipper**

A pretty group known as the Little Guys,
these miniature hybrids produce numerous
flowers on compact plants and can be
relied on to bloom several times a year.
They may become almost perpetually
blooming, with new flower spikes produced
before the last has lost its blooms. The
main colouring within this group is pink,
or pink and white, with deeper red lips.
The gracefully arching flower spikes
become pendent if unsupported; the main
flowering peaks in autumn and winter.

FLOWER
5cm (2in) wide

FLOWER SPIKE
23cm (9in) long

POT SIZE
12cm (5in)

PLANT SIZE
15cm (6in)

TEMPERATURE
Warm

Phalaenopsis **Brother Buddha**

The Brother hybrids are the result of a
huge wave of hybridizing in Taiwan, this
one raised in 1992 by Brothers Orchid
Nursery. The yellow-flowered hybrids
produce smaller flowers but their reduced
size is more than made up for by their
lovely colouring and patterning. The
plants are compact and the flower spikes
shorter, with less flowers on a spike. The
blooms are displayed horizontally, rather
than drooping on long arching spikes
as in the white, pink and red varieties.

FLOWER
6cm (2⅓in) wide

FLOWER SPIKE
25cm (10in) long

PLANT SIZE
30cm (12in) high

POT SIZE
12cm (5in)

TEMPERATURE
Warm

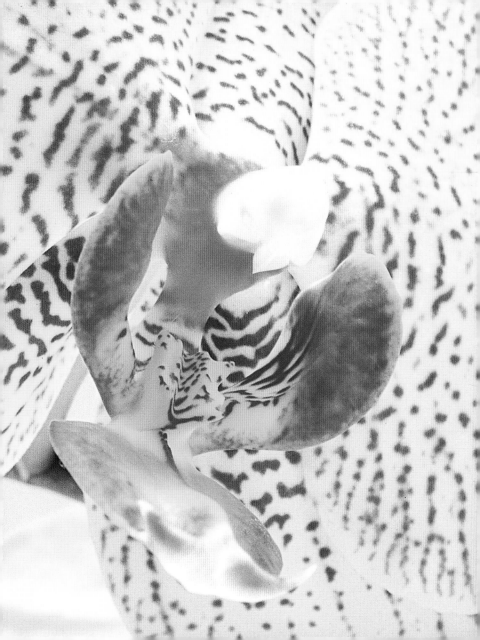

Phalaenopsis **Hawaiian Darling**

This delightful modern hybrid was raised in Hawaii, where many new variants are emerging. The marking comes through as rosy-mauve spotting on the lower sepals, partially hidden by the well-rounded petals. The basically white flower has a slight pink flush retained from the pink hybrid parent. The arching habit of the spike naturally arranges the blooms in a descending spray. The plant blooms 2-3 times a year, the flowers lasting for several weeks.

FLOWER
6cm (2½in) wide

FLOWER SPIKE
75cm (30in) long

PLANT SIZE
30cm (12in) high

POT SIZE
12cm (5in)

TEMPERATURE
Warm

Phalaenopsis **Lipperose**

This delicately-coloured German-bred
hybrid was raised in 1968, the forerunner
of a long line of pink-flowered hybrids now
popular around the world. Ahead of its
time, it was regarded as a breakthrough in
the breeding of quality phalaenopsis,
previously led by the whites. The soft hues
are retained from the original species.
A well-grown plant which misses a
flowering can be encouraged to bloom by
lowering the minimum temperature
for a few weeks, which will usually initiate
the flower spike into activity.

FLOWER
8cm (3in) wide

FLOWER SPIKE
30cm (12in) long

PLANT SIZE
30cm (12in) high

POT SIZE
12cm (5in)

TEMPERATURE
Warm

Phalaenopsis **Yellow Treasure**

P. Yellow Treasure is an example of the clear yellow hybrids available to those who prefer plain, simple flowers. It is one of the latest yellow hybrids to come from the Pacific rim, now exporting to a worldwide market. Yellow-flowered *Phalaenopsis* vary from almost white, with pale yellow radiating out from the centre, to the deep, self-coloured hybrids which assume an almost golden tinge. They contrast sharply with lime-coloured flowers, which look cool on the hottest day.

FLOWER
8cm (3in) wide

FLOWER SPIKE
30cm (12in) long

PLANT SIZE
30cm (12in) high

POT SIZE
12cm (5in)

TEMPERATURE
Warm

Phalaenopsis **Follett**

In this beautiful hybrid the petal decoration of delicate veining and stripes has been taken to its full potential and the well-shaped flowers are enhanced by the deeper coloured lip. The Californian-bred hybrid, raised in 1993, is the result of a long line of specialized breeding to produce these popular orchids often sold under the name 'candy stripes'. Mature plants produce long, branching flower spikes whose blooms open from the lowest on a stem to the buds at the end in less than a week.

FLOWER
8cm (3in) wide

FLOWER SPIKE
75cm (30in) long

PLANT SIZE
30cm (12in) high

POT SIZE
12cm (5in)

TEMPERATURE
Warm

Phalaenopsis **Hisa Lady Rose**

P. Hisa Lady Rose, raised in 1988, is the
latest in a long line of Japanese-bred
plants. In this hybrid a beautifully shaped
bloom of pure colour combines grace with
quality, while the intricate detail of the inner
lip gives a clear indication to pollinating
insects on how to proceed. Treated with
care, phalaenopsis will live for many
years without growing too large or hard
to handle. Their size is self-regulating
as older leaves are shed to make way for
new ones forming in the plant's centre.

FLOWER 10cm (4in) wide
FLOWER SPIKE 75cm (30in) long
PLANT SIZE 30cm (12in) high
POT SIZE 12cm (5in)
TEMPERATURE Warm

Phalaenopsis **Fajen's Fireworks**

This hybrid was first produced by the Florida nursery, Fajen's Orchids and Exotics, in 1991, following a French line of breeding. The line veining throughout the petals, breaking up into delicate spotting on the lower sepals, forms the perfect backdrop to the intensified lip colour which is this orchid's main feature.

FLOWER
8cm (3in) wide

FLOWER SPIKE
45cm (18in) long

PLANT SIZE
30cm (12in) high

POT SIZE
12cm (5in)

TEMPERATURE
Warm

Phalaenopsis **Miss Print**

Light striping over a pale base
contrasts with the cherry-red lip in
this popular, well-shaped hybrid.
Those hybrids which contain both
pink and white in their blooms
remain the most popular among
beginners' orchids. So many have
been raised for the pot plant market
that you will see many similar
varieties bearing different names.

FLOWER 8cm (3in) wide
FLOWER SPIKE 45cm (18in) long
PLANT SIZE 30cm (12in) high
POT SIZE 12cm (5in)
TEMPERATURE Warm

Phalaenopsis **Petite Snow**

Selective breeding from small species has resulted in a much reduced flower, produced in quantity on a compact spike. This gem combines the qualities of the larger types in cheerful rosy-pink colourings; it is ideal where space is limited, or for a larger collection. The flowers all open together on the spike, which arches naturally and needs little support. It is not unusual for this type to produce more than one flower spike at a time, giving an excellent show of blooms for its size.

FLOWER
5cm (2in) wide

FLOWER SPIKE
23cm (9in) long

PLANT SIZE
15cm (6in) high

POT SIZE
12cm (5in)

TEMPERATURE
Warm

Phalaenopsis **Sweet Memory**

These individual flowers are richly coloured, with darker overtones on a light base, contrasting with the deep red of the lip. The blooms have a heavier texture and a more open shape than more conventional *Phalaenopsis* hybrids. The plants can become large-leaved, producing tall, branching flower spikes to give a wonderful show; summer is the peak flowering period.

FLOWER
8cm (3in) wide

FLOWER SPIKE
60cm (24in) long

PLANT SIZE
38cm (15in) high

POT SIZE
15cm (6in)

TEMPERATURE
Warm

Phalaenopsis **Pink Twilight**

This appealing flower is typical of the hybrids raised using successive generations of pink Philippines species. Pink Twilight has showy blooms, the flowers arranged neatly along two sides of the stem. The stem arches under its own weight as the flowers open: the blooms are produced 2-3 times a year and last for weeks. The intricate detail of the lip reveals the minute decoration, and mysterious shape, which spell out a message to the pollinating insect. Hybridizing has greatly enhanced the lip decoration.

FLOWER
8cm (3in) wide

FLOWER SPIKE
30cm (12in) long

PLANT SIZE
30cm (12in) high

POT SIZE
12cm (5in)

TEMPERATURE
Warm

Phalaenopsis **San Luca**

The unusual rich red colouring of this fine hybrid was achieved only by the dedication of the hybridizers, in this instance in California where young plants can be brought to flowering size in the shortest possible time. The splash-petal effect behind the candy-striped veining is offset by the ruby-red lip. The large blooms are produced on the end of tall flower spikes with nodes; once the initial flowering is over, further branches of flowers can be activated by cutting the end of the stem back to a lower node.

FLOWER
10cm (4in) wide

FLOWER SPIKE
75cm (30in) long

PLANT SIZE
30cm (12in) high

POT SIZE
12cm (5in)

TEMPERATURE
Warm

Phalaenopsis **Golden Bells**

This pretty variety has distinct deep yellow dotting over a pale yellow ground, which makes a pleasing, unusual combination. The russet-red highlight at the centre of the white lip gives the whole flower a bright appearance. Yellow hybrids produce slightly smaller flowers which keep their colour through the long period of bloom, and the more compact flower spike remains upright without a supporting cane, making this an ideal plant to grow where space is limited.

FLOWER 6cm (2½in) wide
FLOWER SPIKE 25cm (10in) long
PLANT SIZE 20cm (8in) high
POT SIZE 12cm (5in)
TEMPERATURE Warm

Orchid Care

The majority of orchids in cultivation are epiphytic plants used to an aerial lifestyle and their roots have evolved accordingly. Even though the cultivated hybrids may be many times removed from the original species through generations of breeding, they retain the same basic plant and root structure, which is what makes the cultivation of orchids different from that of most other plants.

Orchid Compost

The first requirements of an orchid compost are that it should be open, well aerated and free-draining. It needs to hold the plant steady in its pot and should retain enough moisture and nutrients for long-term absorption by the roots. It must also be slow to decompose, reasonably easy and pleasant to use and readily available. The most widely used organic material which fits all these attributes is pine or fir bark chippings.

There are several variations on this bark-based compost. For example, a proportion of peat may be added, increasing its moisture-holding qualities, which is an advantage for some orchids with thick-rooting systems, such as *Cymbidium*. It is also useful for busy growers who may be unable to tend to the watering of their plants often, and need them to stay wet for longer periods. Other organic materials used as a substitute for peat include beech husks, coir and tree fern fibre. All these composts are available in large garden centres and specialist nurseries.

A number of man-made materials make good, if unlikely, orchid composts. These include Rockwool, an artificially made fibre with all the qualities of a good compost, except that it is inert so cannot contribute any nutrients. The advantages of this type of material are that the plant can be kept wetter without any danger of infection or rot setting in and, as there is no slow decomposition, the compound does not alter over the years. The disadvantage is that it becomes necessary to supply the plants with exactly the right amount of feed in a balanced combination to maintain steady growth. Two types of Rockwool are available, absorbent and water-repellent. They can be mixed together or used separately, depending on the moisture retention needed.

A number of other inert materials are suitable for orchids, used either on their own or combined with a bark mixture: these include horticultural foam – a mix of foam sponge and dried moss – and expanded clay pellets. Both of these are absorbent, help to retain moisture and allow air to circulate around the roots. Any potting material should be soaked beforehand and used in a dampened state. Bone-dry compost is difficult to work with and will take a long time to absorb water; this could harm a newly potted plant by retarding the growth of its new roots.

When deciding on the best compost for your orchids, be advised by the nursery that supplied them. Try to keep all your orchids in the same type of mix, but if after some time a plant is not doing well, consider changing to another compost. However, avoid constantly changing composts in the hope of reviving an ailing plant, as the cause of its ill health may lie elsewhere and continually disturbing its roots will make matters worse. (For potting up orchids, see Repotting, page 297.)

Watering

Orchids are slow-growing plants and many live for years, following a regulated pattern of growing and resting cycles. While the plants are growing they need to be kept evenly moist at the roots, without the compost becoming either too wet or too dry. The open nature of orchid compost should ensure that water drains through the pot within seconds, retaining just enough for the roots to absorb.

Watering probably causes more concern to the beginner than any other aspect of growing orchids as the unfamiliar pseudobulbs and unusual compost do not make it obvious when the orchid is in need of water. And while the surface of the compost may look dry, it can be quite wet underneath. Lifting the plant to test whether it feels light is a good way to decide and, if you are still unsure, weigh the plants on the kitchen scales! This will help you get an initial idea of how often to water until you have more experience.

Both overwatering and underwatering can cause problems. If too much water stays in the compost over a period of time, an organic compost such as bark will stagnate and decompose, causing the roots to die from lack of air. Orchid roots are valuable and, once lost, it can take time for new ones to be made. Each pseudobulb develops its own roots at the start of the growing season and the plant has to survive on these until the next new growths are active and can produce their own roots.

Older pseudobulbs which have lost their roots are unlikely to make new ones and will simply shrivel. If your orchids are in a man-made compost, there is far less danger of roots rotting; they can safely be kept in a perpetually wet state without risk of overwatering.

Plants that have been underwatered over a long period will simply stop growing roots, and those in the pot will eventually dry up and die. Once the roots stop taking up water for storage in the pseudobulbs, these will shrivel as reserves are used up. Shrivelled pseudobulbs can therefore be the result of either under- or overwatering, but a close look at the state of the compost will quickly determine the likely cause. And while the underwatered plant will recover after a good soak, an overwatered one will need careful repotting and attention over a long period before it recovers fully.

The amount of water to give at each application varies according to the individual orchid. A plant which has filled its pot with a solid rootball or has pushed itself out of the pot will be difficult to water because most of the liquid will run off over the edge. If only a little penetrates the compost, it may appear wet on top but still be dry underneath. This is especially true of thick-rooting cymbidiums, which can become potbound after a couple of years. On the other hand, a newly potted plant, surrounded by fresh compost and with a less developed root system, can easily be overwatered. The best way to water a newly potted plant is by flooding the surface several times until it retains enough water to soak right through to the bottom of the pot. The smaller the pot, the more often it will need watering.

Water orchids from the top, using a long-spouted can and pouring water over and all around the surface of the compost. Take care not to wash pieces of bark over the rim. It will do no harm to splash water onto the mature pseudobulbs and let it run down between them, but make sure you do not allow water into the funnel of a growing pseudobulb, or the central leaf of a *Paphiopedilum*, which can cause basal rot.

The easiest way to water orchids is to take the plants into the kitchen, where you can place them on a draining board and allow surplus water to drain away. This avoids the danger of orchids being left standing in a saucer of water, which prevents the base of the plant drying out at the same time as the top, which could be detrimental to the roots. If the orchids are to be watered in situ, stand them on upturned saucers or half-pots in a tray deep enough for surplus water not to spill onto the floor.

The best time to water orchids is while the temperature is rising. In summer and in warm weather this can be at any time of day, but in winter, when the temperature may not rise much at all, water only in the morning. By the time temperatures start to drop in late afternoon or evening, all surplus water should have dried up. In summer, you will need to give more water because the plants are actively growing and transpiring, while some water is lost to evaporation.

Aim to check your plants almost daily: you should expect to water once or twice a week, depending on the state of the compost. In winter, some orchids will be resting and others growing more slowly. Slow-growing orchids need to be kept just slightly moist, so water them occasionally. Those that are resting need only enough water to prevent the pseudobulbs from shrivelling, or none at all.

Use water at room temperature. If you collect mains or rain water in an outside butt, keep a small supply indoors for immediate use. Orchids prefer soft water and in some areas, where the mains supply is hard, it may be an advantage to collect rain water. But in urban areas, where rain water is contaminated with pollutants, water from the tap is safer. Water used to create humidity can be taken straight from the mains, but you should avoid spraying orchids with hard water as it may leave a coating of limescale on the leaves.

Feeding

 In the wild, epiphytic orchids are deluged daily throughout their growing season, but drying winds and the sun which follows heavy rain ensure that they are soon dry again. With each down-pour, water is washed down the bark of the trees, bringing with it meagre nutrients in the form of bird or animal droppings and decomposing leaf litter which settles around the roots and at the base of the orchids. In this way the plants receive additional nourishment, but they remain essentially light feeders.

In cultivation you must apply artificial feed according to the type of compost. Bark chippings are a slowly decomposing material, releasing a steady food supply over a long period which, in itself, is sufficient for some orchids. Those growing in modern man-made composts are totally dependent on artificial feed for their nourishment. It is best to feed orchids lightly as more harm can be done through overfeeding, causing the roots to be burnt by a build-up of chemicals in the compost.

Balanced orchid feed is available in liquid or granular form through specialist nurseries and garden centres. The liquid feed comes in concentrated form and the recommended dosage often requires it to be diluted into litres of water so that, if you only have a few plants, too much has to made up at a time. Do not be tempted to re-use the rest of this amount over a long period – mix a new solution for each feeding and discard any remainder. Do not keep a bottle of liquid feed for more than one season as it may change its chemical composition slightly over time. Granular feed can be made up in smaller quantities, with none going to waste.

Orchid feed can be either nitrate- or phosphate-based. Nitrate-based feeds promote growth and should be applied at the start of the growing season and continued until growth is fully developed. Phosphate-based feeds are used to encourage flowering in a plant which has completed its growing. Once the pseudo-bulb is forming and maturing, but before flower spikes are visible, discontinue the nitrate-based feed and apply phosphate-based feed right through the flowering season; do not attempt to force a plant into flowering before its time.

The best way to apply feed is to water the solution into the pot, directly from the top. Only healthy orchids should be given feed. Sick plants which have lost their roots have no means of taking up the extra nutrients. Always apply feed when the compost is moist. Adding feed to a dry pot can prevent it dispersing properly, which again might damage the roots. Orchids that are otherwise healthy, but whose foliage has a yellowish colour, may be suffering from a lack of nutrients; in this case it can be beneficial to spray the foliage lightly with diluted feed to restore it to a healthy green.

There is no need to apply feed every time a plant is watered. To prevent the build-up of unwanted salts in the compost, give at least one watering with clear water in between each feed. This will flush the compost and ensure that all unwanted fertilizer is washed through.

Orchids need to be fed only while growing and active. The start of the growing season depends on the individual orchid. Begin feeding as soon as active growth is seen, with new roots at the base, and continue through the summer, gradually lessening in autumn. Discontinue feeding entirely by the onset of winter. Once the growing season is over and the plant is resting or has slowed down growth, discontinue feeding any deciduous orchids, such as *Pleione*, and reduce feed for *Cymbidium* and *Odontoglossum*.

Spraying and Humidity

Spraying orchids is not a substitute for watering but an additional part of their care; it should be a daily routine. Spray using a hand-held bottle, wetting the foliage enough to allow small droplets of water to remain on the leaves, but not so much that the surplus runs down them. Lightly mist all parts of the plant, including underneath, but avoiding any flowers. In summer this will help to cool the foliage as well as keeping the leaves dust-free.

Evergreen orchids such as *Cymbidium*, *Odontoglossum* and *Cattleya* can be liberally sprayed for most of the year, while deciduous kinds, including *Pleione*, should be hardly sprayed at all – their softer foliage will become spotted if water is allowed to lie on it for several hours at a time. A light misting on sunny days is sufficient. *Phalaenopsis* and *Paphiopedilum* should be misted only lightly, so water does not run down the centre of their growth.

Humidity is synonymous with good orchid culture as it helps to provide the right atmosphere. The surrounding humidity should always balance the temperature. Provided plants are kept evenly moist at the roots while they are growing, they will not suffer from a lack of humidity. Where the orchids stand on humidity trays filled with pebbles or expanded clay pellets which are topped up with water, there will be enough moisture rising up to create a microclimate. Indoor growing cases can be fitted with humidity trays in the same way. Humidity becomes significantly more important indoors in winter, when central heating dries the air faster, so spraying to maintain humidity can continue throughout most of the year.

The hardest place to achieve a balance between humidity and temperature is a conservatory. Light usually comes in from more than one direction, increasing the temperature fluctuation, and orchids grown here may suffer from a dry atmosphere. If they remain in a conservatory all summer, you should spray vigilantly and use humidity trays where possible.

Light and Shade

Orchids need light but not full sun. Their leaves have adapted over millions of years to thrive in the dappled shade provided by the tree canopy of their natural environment. In the home, light usually enters a room from one direction only, so there is little danger of orchids being exposed to too much light unless they are standing directly in the sun close to a south-facing window. Shade can easily be provided by net curtains, slatted blinds or an outside sun blind. Provided the sun is not shining directly onto the foliage at midday in the summer, most orchids can benefit from early morning or late afternoon and evening sun, when the rays reach the leaves at a low enough angle not to harm them.

Orchids like *Cymbidium, Dendrobium* and *Coelogyne* can take more direct light than others. *Phalaenopsis* and *Paphiopedilum* require the most shade, and these should always be kept away from the window or stood behind other plants to afford them extra shade. Cattleyas are often thought to tolerate high light levels, but they can suffer more than most from direct sun, which can quickly burn the fleshy leaves.

In winter, orchids should be given all the light available. Most orchids are resting during this time as it is the season for ripening the pseudobulbs and growths made the previous summer. The most dangerous time is early spring when the sun is gaining in power daily, and the orchids, having not been exposed to sun all winter, can suffer from an excess of light. It is wise to put shading in position before the danger of over-exposure to sun.

Orchids can be given separate summer and winter quarters to take into account the light they receive. While a south- or west-facing aspect may be ideal in winter, this would give too much sun in summer. Either move them to an east- or north-facing window for summer, or leave them where they are if shading is provided. Bear in mind that outside trees or hedges may provide partial shade in summer.

Aim to keep the foliage a good healthy green colour. The leaves of orchids under stress from being exposed to too much light or direct sun will turn yellowish or reddish. If the sun burns a leaf, this will appear as a black or brown area on the surface directly facing the sun. Orchids which have been kept too heavily shaded or in a poorly lit area of the home will have darker green foliage, lacking lustre or gloss. The leaves will be long and lank and the pseudobulbs will have ripened insufficiently to produce a flower spike.

Temperature

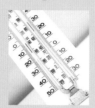 For cultivation purposes, orchids are neatly divided into three groups of temperature tolerance, depending on where the original species originates in the wild. The altitude at which orchids are found is more important than their global position, and whether they grow high in the tree canopy or near the base of the tree in leaf litter. Wherever orchids are found growing naturally, even in tropical parts of the world, the temperature can drop considerably at night; this cooling down period helps them to cope with several hours of higher daytime temperatures. There is also a temperature variation between summer and winter, and warm and cool days in each season, depending on the weather and hours of sunshine. Therefore it is quite natural, indeed essential, for orchids to experience fluctuations of temperature from day to day. A comfortable temperature range between which orchids can be grown is 10–30°C (50–85°F), a range which encompasses the needs of almost all cultivated orchids.

Orchids exposed to higher or lower temperatures than this over a prolonged period will show signs of stress, although the occasional hot day or cold night will not harm them. One of the most useful pieces of equipment is a maximum/minimum thermometer. This will record the rise and fall in temperature when you are away, or at night.

If orchids are exposed to extremes of temperature over a long period, their performance is affected and their growth will slow down until it ceases altogether. Those exposed to below recommended temperatures in winter take longer to produce new growths in spring and also suffer from leaf loss. Orchids kept too warm in summer will respond by not producing flowers, though their growth may appear normal.

Most orchids in cultivation are cool-growing, including *Cymbidium*, *Coelogyne*, *Odontoglossum* and many more. They need a minimum night temperature of 10°C (50°F) and a maximum daytime summer temperature of 24°C (75°F). Intermediate orchids need a winter minimum temperature of 13°C (55°F), with a summer daytime maximum of 30°C (85°F). Warm-growing orchids need a minimum winter night temperature of 18°C (64°F), with a summer daytime maximum of 32°C (90°F).

Orchids in these three groups should ideally be kept in separate rooms, to meet their individual temperature needs. The main difference in temperature will be at night in winter. In summer, there will be little variation between daytime temperatures which depend on natural conditions.

To maintain a high enough winter temperature, artificial heating will usually be needed. Most homes are sufficiently warm and a conservatory can easily be heated by running an extra radiator from the central heating system. Do not keep cool-growing orchids too warm at night as this will affect their flower production. The same risk occurs if intermediate or warm-growing orchids are kept too cold.

Repotting and Dividing

Adult orchids are generally repotted every two years in spring, at the start of their growing season. Repotting involves removing the plant from its pot, discarding all the old compost, trimming the roots and returning it to a larger pot in fresh compost. When repotting a mature orchid that has outgrown its pot, you may consider dividing it to form several new plants, rather than simply increasing the pot size. Young orchids and divisions are 'dropped on' every six months, in spring and early autumn. Dropping on is when a young plant is carefully taken from one pot and placed into a larger one without disturbing the rootball; it is used when the existing compost does not need replacing.

A plant is in need of repotting when the compost has deteriorated and is clogged with decomposing particles. If you can push a finger through the compost, this indicates that it has broken down, has no food value left and is no longer aerated. Left in this compost, a plant will quickly lose its roots as water does not drain through and the compost becomes sodden. Plants also need repotting when there is no room in the pot for further growth to be made, or when the roots have become so cramped that the plant has pushed itself above the rim. A further reason is when a plant has become sick through incorrect watering and needs urgent attention to its roots. Do not repot orchids which are flowering or resting – wait until new growth shows.

The aim of every orchid grower is to keep the plants in harmony and balance which, in the case of most evergreen orchids, is when there are several pseudo-bulbs in full leaf. As these orchids age, they shed their leaves – usually one or two in a season – until none are left, at which stage the pseudo-bulb is termed a 'back bulb'. Back bulbs retain food reserves and can be propa-gated to make new plants. An orchid should always have more pseudobulbs in leaf than out of leaf but where, over a period, several have lost their foliage, you should cut off all surplus back bulbs, or they will restrict new growth and successive pseudobulbs will start to get smaller.

Orchids which produce more than one new growth, or lead, will grow in different directions at once and these plants can be divided, provided that at least four pseudobulbs, mostly in leaf, can be left on each division. Never divide a plant into pieces smaller than four pseudobulbs each or you will prevent it from flowering for at least another year. You can of course leave plants intact if you are grow-ing them on into specimen size, provided there are always more pseudobulbs with

leaves than not, to keep the balance. Pseudobulbs are attached by a strong rhizome which is usually below the surface and not easily visible.

Orchids without pseudobulbs do not extend outwards to fill their pots but need repotting when the compost has deteriorated, or when they have been in the same pot for more than two years. Tall-growing orchids can become top-heavy and by the time their pots are full of roots they need a larger container. Shorter-growing orchids, particularly *Phalaenopsis*, are mostly dropped on to avoid disturbing the roots. If the compost has decomposed, replace it before return-ing the orchid to the same size container.

REPOTTING

Before you start repot-ting, lay down a few sheets of newspaper to collect old compost and dead roots. Have ready a supply of dampened compost, preferably wetted the previous day, a selection of larger-size pots and a supply of crocking material for drainage, such as pieces of polystyrene. You will also need scissors, secateurs or a sharp pruning knife; these tools should be sterilized, so have a lighter or a bottle of methylated spirits handy and flame or clean the tool after each use. Wear disposable gloves if you are using a man-made fibre such as Rockwool or horticultural foam.

1 Remove the orchid from its pot by holding it upside down and tapping the edge of the pot against the worktop. If the plant is not rootbound it will slide out easily. Where there is a thick ball of roots, simply run the pruning knife around the inside rim to loosen them.

2 Lay the plant on the paper and examine its roots: they should be white and firm to the touch, with active growing tips. Cut off any that are blackened and hollow after teasing the roots apart. Dead roots may be wet and soggy or, if they have dried out, the outer covering will pull away to reveal an inner wire-like core. If all roots look white and healthy and the plant does not need to be divided, just slip it into a pot about 5cm (2in) larger.

3 Place a layer of crocks at the bottom of the pot for drainage then put in a little compost. Place the orchid on top of this, with the oldest pseudobulbs against one side of the pot, allowing as much space as possible between the new growths and the rim: this is the direction in which the plant will continue to grow.

4 Hold the plant firmly, with the base of the new growth level with the top of the pot and pour new compost around the plant until it is steady. Firm bark compost well but do not press Rockwool-type compost down so hard. The pseudobulbs should 'sit' comfortably on the surface, 2.5cm (1in) from the top of a pot, to allow for watering the plant without washing compost over the edge.

Orchids such as *Phalaenopsis*, which have a number of aerial roots outside the pot, can be repotted in this way but without placing the aerial roots in the compost. Having developed in the air, they would suffocate and die if transferred to the container. Repot carefully so as not to break the aerial roots. Give the plants a few days to allow damaged roots to heal, then water sparingly; resume normal watering a week later. Spray the leaves often to reduce moisture loss.

DIVIDING LARGE ORCHIDS

1 When repotting a large plant which needs dividing or its back bulbs reducing, remove it from the pot and decide where to divide it. Push the pseudobulbs apart with your fingers and thumb where you intend to make the split and, using a pruning knife, sever the rhizome between the pseudobulbs. Cut right through the rootball until the two parts are separated.

2 Remove all old or decayed compost from the main part of the plant, then tease out the roots, trimming back any dead and broken ones with secateurs or scissors to the base of the plant. Trim the live roots to 15cm (6in) or so long. Orchids do not make permanent roots and, while this action may seem drastic, it simply stimulates the plant to make new roots and allows more space in the container for them to grow.

3 The main portion of the plant may now be returned to the same size container, or possibly a slightly larger one, making sure there is a 5cm (2in) gap for it to grow into. Hold the plant steady and fill around it with compost. Firm it down well to hold the plant securely.

4 Where a plant has been divided into equal portions, repot the other divisions in the same way, using a pot of the right size. Any leafless back bulbs that have been removed will have no live roots, these having died naturally when the leaves were shed. If you wish to use back bulbs for propagating, divide them up singly, reserving only those which are plump and green. Trim back the dead roots, leaving just enough to anchor each back bulb in its container, and pot them into separate small pots or place them round the edge of a large container. Discard the older, shrivelled back bulbs, as they will have insufficient reserves left to grow.

Keeping Orchids Healthy

A healthy orchid should have good-sized, plump pseudobulbs, increasing rather than decreasing in size, with the largest at the front. The newest pseudobulbs are the most significant and it is acceptable for the oldest ones at the back to have shrivelled through old age. In evergreen orchids, like *Cymbidium*, most of the pseudobulbs should carry healthy leaves of a good green colour and be neither limp nor dehydrated. There should be an abundance of live roots: check by slipping the plant out of its pot without disturbing the compost. In *Phalaenopsis* the leaves should be firm and a good mid-green, not pitted or dehydrated, with active roots showing around the pot or over the side. There should never be less than three leaves at any time.

A sickly plant will show signs of stress. The following points will help you to diagnose the problem.

■ Yellowing or reddening of the foliage may indicate too much light in summer or a lack of fertilizer: place the plant in a shadier position and increase the feed until the leaves return to a good green.

■ Premature leaf loss, where an evergreen orchid loses most or all of its foliage at once, may be caused by overwatering, severe temperature fluctuations or a combination of harmful conditions. To return such an orchid to good health can take years, so it is often better to improve growing conditions and replace the plant.

■ Shrivelled pseudobulbs or leaves on *Cattleya*, *Phalaenopsis* and others with fleshy foliage may indicate dehydration, caused by over- or underwatering. An overwatered plant will have lost its roots through being kept too wet and will need careful treatment to restore it to health. Repot in fresh compost to encourage new roots to develop. Underwatered plants need more water at the base. Soaking in a bucket of water for half an hour plumps up shrivelled pseudobulbs within a week.

■ Black tips at the ends of leaves are a sign of an imbalance of cultural factors. Trim back the tips with a sterilized tool and re-position the plant. Black patches on a leaf may be sunburn, where the burn relates to the sun's position on the leaf surface. The disfigurement will not return to green, so remove that part of the leaf.

Orchids in a sickly state are unlikely to flower, unless they are so weakened that they use their last reserves to bloom before they die. The best advice is to enjoy the flowers while they last, then replace the plant. Orchids which appear healthy but do not flower are probably being grown too soft, in conditions that are too warm or where the temperature drops insufficiently at night. Keeping cool-growing orchids in too warm a night temperature or under too heavy shade can result in lush growth unable to produce a flower spike. Lower the temperature to encourage flowering next season.

Phalaenopsis can benefit from a seasonal lowering of the night-time temperature by up to 10°C (14°F) for 2-3 weeks at a time, which usually encourages a flower spike to appear. But most orchids have a defined flowering season and should not be encouraged to bloom at other times. Orchids which have missed flowering for a few years but remain healthy should bloom freely once conditions permit. The flower spikes of *Odontoglossum*, *Cymbidium* and others which produce a heavy crop of flowers can kink or snap under their own weight as blooms develop, so tie them to a bamboo cane for support.

Inspect your plants daily to ensure they are watered and give their leaves a daily spray or sponge to keep them fresh and dust-free. Watch out for emerging flower spikes and mark their position with a short cane to prevent them breaking. Tall flower spikes need support as they grow, but you should leave the flowering part of a long spray free to arch naturally. As the flowers fade on the spike, remove them before they drop; cut old spikes down to the base. *Phalaenopsis* are an exception and, provided the plant is strong and growing well, it may support a secondary flower spike from a stem. To encourage prolonged flowering, cut the finished spike back to a lower node.

Pests and Diseases

Orchids growing within a clean indoor environment are unlikely to be bothered by many pests or diseases, but a few pests, if left undetected, can build up into sizeable colonies that are hard to eradicate. In most cases there is no need to resort to using chemical control.

Greenfly is the most likely pest. These sap-sucking insects enter through open windows in spring and summer and will settle on buds and new growths, causing blemishes on young leaves and deformities on buds. They also excrete a sugary substance which can stick to the leaf, on which sooty mould will grow. When you see greenfly, rinse them off in water; use a small paintbrush to dislodge those left.

Pests harder to detect include red spider mite, scale insects and mealybug. Red spider mite thrives on the undersides of leaves and likes the dry conditions of the home. Because it is so small you will usually notice the damage first – a silvery white mottling on the leaves, caused where this sap-sucking pest has attacked the leaf. To control, treat all foliage with insecticidal soap (available from garden centres in a ready-to-use spray). Do this weekly until both pest and eggs have gone. The white mottling can turn black as a fungal infection spreads into dead leaf cells.

Scale insects, up to 3mm (⅛in) long, may be hard or soft. Adults cover themselves with a white or brown shell and remain in one position on the leaf, moving on only after a yellow patch appears. They can be hard to dislodge and may have to be scrubbed from the leaf with a toothbrush dipped in insecticidal soap. The young move around the plant so it may take several efforts to eradicate scales.

Mealybug is up to 3mm (⅛in) long, with a flat, oval shape. It covers its pinkish body with a white mealy substance and sucks sap from the leaf, leaving yellow patches where it has been. Look for this pest in the inaccessible places between leaves and beneath bracts. Remove using a cotton bud dipped in insecticidal soap.

Disease in orchids is usually the result of neglect over a long period, subjecting a plant to stress which makes it vulnerable. The most common disease is cymbidium mosaic virus which shows up on new leaves as white flecking, which later turns black from fungal infection. The means of transmission is unknown but there is no cure for this virus. If you suspect a plant of being infected, keep it away from others until you are sure it is not, or it dies.

The leaves of *Phalaenopsis* and green pseudobulbs of *Odontoglossum* may be affected by a bacterial disease that appears as a watery blemish and dries to leave a brown depression. Remove the affected part then apply sulphur powder.

Index